About Thi

"This is an excellent guide to making inspired decisions. The examples are clear, techniques effective and results immediate."

> *Maxine Haft, Ph.D.,*
> *Clinical Psychologist, New York*

"It's hard to believe the effortlessness and speed with which this approach produces decisions. A whole area of my life – worrying about what to do or about decisions already made – has been cut back almost entirely."

> *Miriam Seidel, Writer and Art Critic,*
> *New York/Philadelphia*

"Dr. Barinov's approach, with its sharp focus on the human element in decisions, is unlike any other approach I know of. It reduces tension, opens up untapped powers and produces wise decisions in complex business situations."

> *Frank Breslin,*
> *Vice-President, Scott Paper Company*

"I use this approach for my career, parenting and all other decisions. It frees me from doubts about being "right" or "wrong. It rewards me with a new self-trust and confidence to move ahead in the changing world."

> *Kathy Dolan, Editor*
> *US/Canadian Biomedical Publications*

This is the first book that shows
how to make instant decisions
in real-life complex situations.

"Once you master the techniques of this book – and they are accessible to all of us -- you obtain a unique control over your business and personal life."

Richard Fluri, Director,
Management Development, Campbell Soup Company

"A road map to success, enjoyable, intelligent and very practical. This book proves that humans are really designed to make instant decisions."

Elizabeth Washburne, Project Manager,
Software Testing, Philadelphia

"Dr. Barinov's approach applies not only to individual decisions but to group decisions as well. I was on a deadlocked jury. I suggested we try one of her techniques, and we quickly came in with a verdict."

Florence Janovic,
Sensible Solutions, Inc., New York

"The techniques are clear, very usable. Applying them keeps me from worrying over decisions."

Elizabeth Frumin, MA,MEd.,
Therapist & Educator, Philadelphia

"If the book's cost deters you, think how much a bad decision costs."

David Reese, CPA,
Information Systems Consultant, Philadelphia

Since learning this approach, I no longer worry about 'what might have been,' because I'm so confident about decisions I make."

Nelly Tsivina, Ph.D.,
Community Health Resources, Greenwich, CT

How to

MAKE INSTANT DECISIONS

and

REMAIN HAPPY & SANE

——

Using Your Inner Compass

Zelma Barinov, Ph. D.

Access Press,

Bala Cynwyd, Pennsylvania

How to Make Instant Decisions and Remain Happy & Sane

Using Your Inner Compass

Published by:

Access Press
P.O. Box 594
Bala Cynwyd, PA 19004-0594

Library of Congress Catalog Card Number: 97-97211
Barinov, Zelma, Ph. D.
       How to Make Instant Decisions and Remain Happy & Sane
             Using Your Inner Compass
       Includes bibliographical references and index.
       ISBN 0-9661071-8-7

Access Press Phone: 610-668-8996, Fax: 610-668-2567,
Email: Accesspres@aol.com

Is This Book For You?

Do you know that *this very moment contains all the information you need for your next step?* More than that, *you can access this information instantly.* How? Through your own inner compass. This book reveals what your inner compass is and how to use it to make instant decisions in complex situations.

If you feel pressured to make right decisions quickly, if you want to know instantly whether you're on the right track, this book may be for you. If you would like to sensitize yourself to subtle warnings against making poor decisions, this book may be for you.

As you read it and apply the new approach, you will be pleasantly surprised to discover that this approach brings to life new decision-making talents you did not know you had. So, *welcome to this new and exhilarating decision-making!*

Table of Contents

1

Your Inner Compass – the Tool for Instant Decisions

Chapters one and two prepare you for using your inner compass. The rest of the book offers scores of ready-to-use techniques for making decisions in any area of your life.

Radically New Decision-Making

Old decision-making has died. The decision-making that relied on "good ol'" logic and let us leisurely study new situations is buried by the current global transformation.

Mankind has entered a "Star Hour" -- a time of monumental transformation, rampant confusion and breathtaking opportunities -- that occurs once in some two thousand years. Inherent in the "Star Hour" is a radically new decision-making to which the old approaches do not apply. That is why, today's decisions challenge us all -- from teenagers to world leaders.

Chapter 1

The world around us is new, very new, even where it appears deceptively familiar. It is as though, instead of handling a familiar machine, we are now facing a sensitive living organism that responds to each move and decision we make, including the moves we deem imperceptible. The responses seem exaggerated, even grotesque, when unintended consequences of our decisions boomerang.

Even the best and the brightest are challenged by these new decision-making conditions:

⇒ The number of options to choose from grows rapidly, ever more options being new. Example: You want to buy an electronic device you liked. But it is no longer manufactured. Instead, you face fifteen new models. New options mushroom also in education, careers, healthcare, insurance, investments, you name it.

⇒ It is no longer possible to predict logically even all major consequences of your decisions. Why? Because the complexity of change defies logic.

⇒ Less and less time is available for making decisions, as the pace of change accelerates. If you linger, you are too late, as rapid change erases your options.

All in all, comparing today's decision-making to that of yesterday is like comparing electronics to horses and buggies, and electronics do not respond well to a horse-and-buggy approach. The new conditions demand that you speed up decision-making a thousandfold. Many think it is beyond human capacities. But what used to be beyond human capacities no longer is. For example, one could not get from New York to San Francisco in hours by horse and buggy. Yet a radically new approach to transportation – traveling through the air by jets -- made it easy. This book presents a radically new approach that lets you decide quickly and easily.

Where will your new quickness and ease come from? They will come from making decisions "holographically." Here is what it means. In holography, an entire image can be restored through its small part when other parts are lacking. Similarly, your inner compass lets you make a decision through whatever bits of information you have available.

> *If you must decide on the spot and cannot get the information you need, your inner compass can still warn you against taking a wrong route.*

That way your inner compass accelerates decision-making a thousandfold. So far humans have been using only a tiny part of the available potential. The inner compass approach plugs you into your richest resource -- your own spirit -- and turns decision-making into an exhilarating and freeing experience.

How the inner compass approach developed.

The approach described here has been developed over the last twenty five years. It started in Russia, where I belonged to the lucky elite of Moscow scientists exploring artificial intelligence and the uses of computers for decision-making. But computers, however great, play a secondary role. The final decisions rest with humans. That is why I refocused my research on the human element in decision-making.

My expertise (in cybernetics and general systems theory) made me aware of the key challenge we face during the "Star Hour" -- to decide ever more quickly in ever more complex situations. I set out to discover how to do that. First, I explored, in collaboration with a prominent psychiatrist, the factors that shaped one's decisions. Then I interviewed people who made brilliant decisions under extreme circumstances, including those who triumphed over death-death (not just life-death) situations.

In life-death situations, there is a chance to survive; in "death-death" situations, there appears to be none. That was the case for political prisoners in a Soviet prison camp located near the Arctic Circle. During the dark and bitterly cold winters, prisoners there labored 12 hours a day, subsisting on a 1/2 lb of rationed bread per day. Tortured by sadistic guards, physically exhausted, they were dying by hundreds from scurvy, pneumonia, and common colds. Disobedience, even minute, was punished with death. Yet one day, a young prisoner, Basil, boldly challenged his captors. He refused to work and sent a letter of complaints to the commandant -- to the very man who supervised the camp. The news spread, and the camp braced for harsh punishment. Instead, something odd happened. Basil was given food and transferred to a room with a bed, blankets, and even -- a luxury unheard of in that nightmarish place -- sheets. Years later, it came to light that shortly before Basil wrote his letter, a squabble had erupted among the camp authorities. His letter fell into the hands of those who were looking for an excuse to dispose of the commandant.

As I probed into Basil's story, I learned that his success was not due to sheer luck. Nor was his decision made out of desperation. Far from it. Indeed, at the time, Basil was twenty years old and full of life. Despite his trials, he was strong physically and psychologically. Why then did he challenge the authorities when, logically, it could bring him only immediate death? He did it because he sensed that somehow it was his winning ticket. Inside him, *a pure exhilaration welled up each time he'd think of writing that letter* to the commandant. It saved his life. His was certainly a brilliant decision.

How does one make brilliant decisions? To my surprise, even the best and the brightest were not quite conscious of their decision-making process. But their stories triggered insights in me. For instance, as I listened to Basil, I felt he had acted as though he had had an antenna tuned to the vibrations of life. Perhaps his clear intention to live to see freedom functioned as such an "antenna."

Let's view the prison camp, with all its prisoners, guards, authorities and facilities, as one system. According to general systems theory,

> *any change in a system reverberates*
> *throughout the entire system.*

In Basil's case, it was the rift among the authorities that reverberated throughout the prison camp, unbeknownst to Basil, producing an opening for him to move away from death. His "antenna" picked up the cue, and his psyche responded.

How can we catch such signals consciously? In search for the answers I researched how great leaders in different parts of the world, different walks of life and dissimilar periods of history had arrived at their great decisions. I began to discover the awareness and skills that help one make instant decisions in complex and unpredictable situations.

That and much more led me to develop my own decision-making approach. I introduced it to my postgraduate students at the Institute for Advanced Studies in Information Science, where I was an associate professor. Leaving Russia and building a new life in the US provided me with splendid opportunities to field-test and fine-tune my approach. I feel I have been given two lifetimes in one, and I am very grateful. My new homeland has enriched the spiritual dimension of my work. My travels among peoples of different cultures have underscored for me decision-making essentials common to all.

Your Inner Compass Is a Team of Five Players & a Coach

Have you noticed that not only leaders of nations but also ordinary folks increasingly find themselves in unexpected situations? We live in unpredictable times. Unpredictable means that when making a decision, you may suddenly find yourself stripped of all the props you took for granted. You may have no access to data, nobody to advise you, no means to get emergency help. Is there anything at all that cannot be stripped away? Yes, there is. One single thing that can never be stripped away is *your own being*. It *is the only decision-making "equipment" you can count on.* Therefore, it warrants careful examination. We start the examination with the logical mind, extolled in the Western world as our main decision-making power.

Contrary to popular belief, the logical mind is slow. The more complex the decision, the more time the logical mind requires to sort things out. As the complexity of life increases, getting the necessary decision-making speed by prodding your mind is as likely as attaining jet speed by whipping a horse. While the logical mind is slow, the following five dimensions of your being broadcast *instant* clues for making decisions:
⇒   your body votes "yea" or "nay" instantly on any decision;
⇒   your imagination lets you glance into future,
⇒   your emotions flash messages and offer "fuel" for action;
⇒   your unconscious mirrors how you are doing, and
⇒   your awareness/intuition deliver instantaneous knowing.
Here is the central point:

As a human, you are equipped with a personal decision-making team, available to you 24 hours a day. There are five players and a coach on your team.

Your five players are your Body and Imagination, your Emotions, Mind and Unconscious. The Coach of the team is your Awareness. Note: we will capitalize the names of team members, but only of *your* team members. When someone else's emotions or, say, the human mind in general are meant, they will not be capitalized.

At this point, you may think: " But the mind, emotions, and other dimensions are so intertwined. I can't separate them!" True, they exert a powerful influence upon each other. However, each retains a distinct, even unique character in decision-making. Similarly, your digestive, endocrine, nervous, and other systems retain their character in bodily functioning even though they are intimately intertwined. As a surgeon must know each bodily system to operate, you must know each team member to make successful decisions. Why? Because

---

your personal decision team -- once you learn to use it --
makes up your inner compass.

See Chart 1.1 at the end of this chapter.

Your inner compass can point your direction as clearly as a magnetic compass points north. But the magnetic compass is primitive compared to your inner compass, which is rich and multidimensional, its dimensions fashioned by the six members of your team. While the magnetic compass is just a box with a needle, your inner compass is, rather, a landscape -- your own decision-making landscape, exciting and ever-changing. Once you learn what the changes in the landscape signal, you will easily make most decisions instantly.

Some people appreciate the inner compass approach immediately. Others resist it. Here is Jay, a manager at a government facility, voicing his objections.

J: It's too complicated to deal with a six-member team.

A: What about a basketball team? Can you leave out any player or the coach?

J: Are you kidding? Each of them is indispensable.

A: Same goes for the decision team. Do you think making decisions is easier than playing basketball?

J: No, of course not.

A: Yet, you pit yourself against your decision team.

J: What do you mean?

A: You see, your team actively participates in your decision-making, whether you are aware of it or not. When you don't use your team players to support you, they undermine your decisions.

J: You sound persuasive. Still, I feel resistant.

A: Welcome to the human race. We all resist the new. But in today's new world, if you keep resisting the new, you will inevitably find yourself trailing behind, embittered and enraged. (Ways to move past resistance are addressed in chapter 9.)

J: How long does it take to learn to play with the team?

A: It depends on you. All techniques in this book are ready to use. Apply them to your current decisions and reap the benefits right away. In case you need first to develop more sensitivity to a certain team member (there are exercises for that), your breakthrough may come a bit later.

It may seem overwhelming to keep up with changes in all six dimensions of your inner compass. Yet we are used to responding to various changes coming at us simultaneously. For instance, when driving, we may listen to the radio while attending to turns in the road, road signs, traffic lights, our passenger's comments and cars that cut in front of us within a hair of our bumper. Of course, beginning drivers may feel overwhelmed. But with practice, simultaneous response to various changes becomes part of the driving routine. The same is true of your inner decision-making landscape. Once you start paying attention to it, important changes in your landscape become as obvious to you as a tractor-trailer is to drivers.

> *Each dimension of your inner compass, i.e., each member of your decision team, is as uniquely vital for decision-making as the heart or liver is for body functioning.*

Each team member broadcasts its own vital decision messages. You can pick them up this very moment, provided you know how. If you don't, read on.

Over 90% of Decision Information Is Nonverbal

At first, a good part of your inner compass may seem imperceptible, because five of its six dimensions deliver nonverbal information. Since our highly verbal culture assigns a central role to verbal interactions, many people don't even realize that

> *Over 90% of communication happens nonverbally and up to 98% (in some cases 100%) of crucial decision-making information is nonverbal.*

Here is an historic example. After World War II, Germany and its capital, Berlin, were divided into East and West. West Berlin was occupied by the Allies -- US, Britain, and France. Vulnerably located in the Soviet-occupied East Germany, West Berlin was supplied by the West through three corridors. In March of 1948, American General Clay wrote from Germany to Washington, D.C. that he perceived a subtle change which gave him a feeling that war may suddenly start. Although he didn't have any data or outward evidence, General Clay em-

17

phasized that his feeling is real (1). Shortly afterward, the Soviets shut the corridors feeding West Berlin. Thanks to General Clay's warning, Washington was able to respond immediately with the first massive airlift in history. Allied airplanes delivered food, coal, and other supplies for two million West Berliners for about a year, until the Soviets lifted the blockade. Had Washington ignored General Clay's message which was *based entirely on nonverbal clues*, a major conflict could have erupted.

How much important nonverbal information do you ignore daily? Can you imagine how it handicaps you to miss 98% of the information needed for your decisions? This book can sensitize you to nonverbal information and help you use it for making instant decisions.

The inner compass approach works for decisions of any nature.

My clients have used it to undergo surgery, sell businesses and open new ones, change life partners, choose clothes, diets, and dates. They have used their inner compass to make wise investments, select new careers, shape a leadership style after major corporate changes, create a new life after a painful divorce, and keep inner peace during corporate downsizing.

I myself have tested every technique presented in this book time and again. One of my own toughest decisions was to become a refugee. In Moscow (Russia), where I was born, I enjoyed a successful career and happy family. I was raised with the notion that the USSR was "a bastion of freedom and hope" that liberated mankind from the nightmare of Hitler and fascism. In the early seventies, I became privy to the findings of a sociologist who had discovered that all along Stalin and Hitler had been mirroring each other's slogans and actions. But Stalin had outdone Hitler. Within the USSR he had exterminated more than twenty million of his own people. The day when I learned that, my world where my country was the "Warrior for the Ideals" exploded. My life had dead-ended. No longer could I hope for freedom in the USSR. Could emigration be a way out? At that time, to apply for emigration meant to lose your job, be publicly derided, threatened, and very likely, beaten and imprisoned. My family did not want that. After all, my husband and I held good jobs, our daughter attended a privileged school, and we lived in a prestigious neighborhood of Moscow. So my loved ones refused even to consider emigration. I felt trapped. At some point, I began to feel as if I had been sitting on a time bomb. My sense of timing (see chapter 9) told me that I must arrive at a decision within ten days. Since my family would not budge, my decision came down to whether I could tear myself away from them and emigrate alone, without friends, connections, language, or money. (It was forbidden to take valuables out of the USSR, even one's own manuscripts.)

Instead of agonizing over that decision, I applied a strategy discussed in chapter 8. I took my daughter and flew to a large blue lake in the high mountains of Soviet Central Asia. There, at a national scientific conference I reported on my latest research. It stirred significant interest and brought me flattering offers to expand my work as I saw fit. After the conference, I journeyed with my daughter to the exotic treasures of Samarkand and Tashkent, then took the train home. As the train was approaching Moscow, the decision came to me with total clarity. I never regretted it, although from the start it challenged me to the utmost.

The first step was to announce to my family that I decided to leave Russia. I dreaded that. What if they refused to join me? Then I would become a pariah not only in society but also in my own family. How would I manage without them in a strange land? And how would my loved ones manage without

Chapter 1

me? At that time Russia was behind the Iron Curtain, and leaving them meant parting forever.

But there was no time to linger. So, I told my family that I'd be very happy if they went with me, but if they did not, I'd have to leave alone. I asked that each of them make whatever decision was right for them. Although my daughter was still a teenager, I felt this was a decision she too had to make on her own.

My husband joined me immediately, and once he did, he never looked back. My daughter's decision was far more trying. She had just started a new school where she was surrounded by exciting new friends. Among them was a man as handsome as a movie star, ten years her senior. They fell in love. When she told him that her parents wanted to leave Russia, he came to us and asked for her hand. He wanted to take the best care of her. So he had already found a full-time job to support her eight years of study to become a pediatrician. It meant he was willing to sacrifice for her his own career. We were touched. We invited him to leave Russia with us. But that he could not do. He was an orphan, and Russia had raised him. He felt he absolutely owed it to Russia to stay there and serve his country.

What was I to do? I love my daughter with all my heart. I could not imagine parting with her. But here they were -- two beautiful young people in love. The decision had to be hers.

Once I applied for permission to emigrate, I lost my job, and nobody could hire me without jeopardizing themselves. Meanwhile, my dear blind mother was subjected to public humiliation because she decided to join me. And that was just the beginning. Had someone followed us with a camera, they would have had a compelling blend of an action movie, tear-jerker and psychological thriller. How did I make it through? I did it with the help of my inner compass. (It was yet incomplete

– it did not include the Body. More on that in chapter 3.) So much for past decisions. What about the future?

What decision-making conditions are in store?

As we enter the Third Millennium, we will face increasingly tough and complex decisions. Everything we value will be at stake. Explosions of information -- ever more staggering, frequent, and unexpected -- will alter the face of our planet. Familiar structures will vanish and new ones will spring into being, only to give way to even newer ones, caused by still another stupendous change.

> *The more challenging the conditions, the more important each member of your inner compass team becomes.*

It's worth repeating that each team member is as vital for decision-making as the heart or liver is for body functioning. But while the healthy heart and liver function superbly when you are blissfully unaware of them, the players on your team do not. The Mind may command a move that the Emotions resent, while the Imagination happily leaves the scene for the beach. Your players act as raw, undisciplined talents, conflicting with each other, unless they are coached and integrated into a winning team.

How to measure the true success of your decisions.

What does it mean to win in decision-making?

> *Decision-making is your Game of Life. The purpose of the Game is to win health, wealth and happiness or, more importantly, to win joy, freedom and peace. When gaining joy, freedom and peace, you are winning. When moving away from them, you are losing.*

21

The awareness of what it means to win in decision-making helps people make instant decisions. Here is my friend Jane, who lost her job when the corporation she worked for relocated. Jane said to me, "I'd like to go to school, but I'm afraid I'm too old for that. What do you think?" I asked, "What do you want most – joy, freedom or peace?" Instantly, she answered, "Peace." I suggested, "Right now, in your imagination go to school. While imagining that, do you feel more peaceful or less? Go with the decision that deepens your peace."

What do joy, freedom and peace mean to you personally? How do you define freedom for yourself? Is it the freedom to be yourself in any situation? Is it the freedom to leave everything behind and, on a moment's notice, start down a new road? The freedom to follow your heart? What expressions of freedom are you personally yearning for?

How do you define peace for yourself? The most practical definition of peace I found is this: "Peace is the cessation of againstness." Indeed, againstness polarizes people; it fosters self-righteousness and hatred. Note how the shift from being *against* (e.g., "I am against violence!") to being *for* ("I am for peaceful resolution of conflicts") deepens inner peace and opens the doors to finding common ground.

In the next chapters we will explore your inner compass and its uses. The rest of this chapter surveys the two main kinds of decisions we make – instant and multiphase ones – and explains the phases through which multiphase decisions unfold.

Instant Vs. Multiphase Decisions

In decision-making -- our Game of Life -- there are times to move with the speed of lightning and there are times to be as still as the hours of dawn. Some decisions -- like getting married, changing jobs and buying houses -- unfold through phases, so we will call them "multiphase decisions." Other decisions must be made instantly. A gloomy example: a menacing figure is approaching you on a dark street. Is the danger real? Decide on the spot -- your life may depend on it.

As the pace of change accelerates, more decisions must be made on the spot, not only to fend off crimes, but simply to stay on top of things. The skills for making multiphase decisions differ from those for making instant decisions, like the skills of paddling in calm waters differ from skills of navigating rapids and waterfalls. But some techniques overlap. To the extent that they do, we will explore multiphase decisions.

Have you ever thought that if you get the right job, marry the right person, become rich or ... (fill in the blank), you would no longer have to face difficult decisions? Idyllic times do not last, however. Inevitably, new discomforts will make another tough decision necessary, and then another, and more after that.

Decision-making is your Game for keeps,

with no time between rounds.

The Right Start and Ending of Decisions.

The decision-making round starts when you recognize the need for a decision. What makes you recognize it? Discomfort does. Indeed, when life moves along smoothly, you don't look for decisions. Only when a change in yourself or circumstances causes strong discomfort, do you recognize the need to decide.

Michael is a case in point. The owner of a fast-growing electronics company, he fell in love with Leslie, a columnist, and got married. After the wedding, Michael's life turned into a roller-coaster ride between the highs of mutual ecstasy and the lows of Leslie's stormy unfounded jealousy. When Michael

23

realized that Leslie's fits of jealousy were not cute displays of affection but her normal behavior, he began to question whether he wanted to remain in the marriage. Michael's discomfort pushed him into a new round of decision-making. First, he needed clarity on what he wanted most in life. His soul-searching confirmed that more than anything he wanted to succeed in business. Would his marriage support him? Counseling revealed that meeting Leslie's mounting demands would leave him time for nothing else, and Michael opted for divorce. Handling the divorce finished this round of decision-making. But the most difficult step for Michael was completing -- letting go of his poignant image of Leslie.

Why you must complete your decisions, why just finishing them isn't enough.

> *In decision-making, "finishing" and "completing" are not synonymous. To "finish" means to bring to an end the implementation of a decision physically. To "complete" means to free your consciousness from this decision, to free all the players on your decision team.*

Harriet's story further illustrates this difference. To keep her business afloat during hard times Harriet had to fire half of her employees. The actual firing finished her decision. But the memories, feelings, and images related to the firing kept haunting her, signaling to her that she had not completed this round of the Game. As long as Harriet's Mind, Imagination, and Emotions were still playing the previous round, they were available only part-time for her current round of the Game. But to win a round, you must give it your 100%!

George provides another example. Ending a torturous relationship with Linda, he finished a round. Then he met June, the woman of his dreams. Yet, in his Imagination, he kept arguing with Linda. Incompletion of that relationship made George unable to win his current round -- to reach happiness and deep intimacy in his new relationship.

> *As we move into the Third Millennium, completion becomes ever more crucial for you as decision-maker. So completion must be included as a paramount phase of any decision.*

To quicken decision-making I introduce another new phase -- "recognize the need for a decision."

Let's break a round of decision-making into these phases:

Phase 1: ***Recognize the need for a decision.*** Do it quickly. How? By paying attention to your discomforts. See chapter 9

Phase 2: ***Commit to a fulfilling goal.*** The key here is being true to yourself (see chapter 10.)

Phase 3: ***Explore available options.*** More on this phase later in this chapter; more on. phases 3-5 in chapters 3-8.

Phase 4: **Select a suitable option**. Do not waste your time on choosing the very best option. Every option has pluses and minuses. Success depends not on the option you choose but on keeping a 100% commitment to your goal until you reach it.

Phase 5: ***Implement and finish***. Be flexible. Keep your eyes on the goal, abandon detours and adopt strategies that increase your joy, freedom, and peace.

Phase 6: ***Completion.*** This is the most important phase where you set yourself free. Completion is detailed in chapter 7. Also, see chart 1.2 at the end of this chapter.

You may want to start a decision-making journal. At the end of the day, write in it one sentence stating what you learned this day that will help you make quick and right decisions. As we proceed, I'll often refer you to your journal.

Audrey's story shows how the six phases may work. Audrey holds an influential administrative position in a prestigious company. When her boss is replaced with a new one whom she hates, she recognizes the need for a decision (phase 1). While searching for a fulfilling goal (phase 2), Audrey becomes aware that she is most happy when writing children's books, where trees sing, birds talk, and magic happens. Should she write full time? As she explores her options (phase 3), she learns that good children's books are in demand and that an equity loan can provide her with enough money for a couple of years. Should she keep her job with its financial rewards or bid farewell to that? In phase 4, Audrey follows her heart, which is with the writing. By submitting her resignation and signing for the loan, she implements her chosen option (phase 5). She lets the previous round vanish like last year's snow (phase 6) and plunges into a new round of decision-making. Over the next year Audrey hardly ever thinks of her old job -- the previous round has been completed. All her players are fully engaged in winning the current one. Her book gets good reviews and indirectly leads to an attractive job offer that Audrey accepts.

How many options you have in your current decision

Think of any decision you need to make. List your options and put the list aside. Now imagine that someone points a gun at you and says, "Give me the information you have or I'll kill you!" How many options do you have? Most people think of two -- to hand over the information or say, "Shoot!" and let the criminal decide your destiny. John Arnold, author of *Make Up Your Mind* suggested five more options. Ben Franklin would negotiate ("Let's talk it over"). John Paul Jones would counterattack, disarm, and capture the criminal. Baron Munchausen, a German adventurer, famous for his tall tales, would say, "Of course, I'll give you information," and then he'd lie. Rip Van

Winkle would stall for time, promising the answer after he sleeps on it, and the lovable Scarecrow of "The Wizard of Oz" would plead ignorance, "I seem to disremember."

When I presented these options to a group of lawyers, they quickly suggested eight more: 8) fake a fit, 9) have a real heart attack and die, 10) swallow your tongue, 11) scream for help, 12) remain silent, 13) distract, e.g., ask, "What brand is your gun?" 14) point out something vital for the criminal ("You're bleeding!"), 15) divert the criminal's attention to someone else: "I don't have this information, but so and so does."

Still more options exist, but 15 are enough to make this key point: Usually, you have many more options than you think. So, the next time you tell yourself, "I have no choice!" remember that *even under the gun, you have at least 15 options. Most likely, you have at least as many options in your current decision* . Write them down now!

Is it better to default or make a wrong decision?

When you actively engage in decision-making, your team gains the experience and insights for your next decisions. What happens when you default? Consider this story. Janice, a legal secretary, thinks the real name of her job is "Boredom Heretofore And Thereafter." She dreams of owning a travel agency. Geography has been her hobby for years. She can describe exotic places most people never heard of as vividly as if they were rooms in her apartment. She loves airports and travel arrangements. When a friend tells Janice about an opening at a travel agency, Janice gets very excited. Then doubts creep in. "What if I'm not qualified enough?" she asks herself. "It is a big and busy agency. They need someone who already knows all the ins and outs. I'm probably too old for them anyway. Besides, they wouldn't pay much to a beginner like me, would they?" To pick herself up, Janice goes to a fine restaurant, then the next night to a movie. By the time she finally calls the agency, they have already hired a new agent. Years later, Janice is still working as a legal secretary.

When you default, as Janice did, you choose inertia. Then, your decision team players go slack in their abilities, like muscles go weak without exercise. Inactive players, having no use for the Coach, pull from the Coach's field of awareness.

Your Unconscious registers decisions by default as incompletions, and they drain your energy (see chapter 7.)

As a rule, we benefit far more from wrong decisions than from defaults, because wrong decisions keep us in practice and enrich us with the accelerated learning device called "mistakes."

Summary

As a human being, you are equipped with an inner compass that gives you the most precious ability to sense a right direction even through the dark fury of a night storm that wrecked your ship, physically or metaphorically. Your inner compass consists of five talented players and a Coach that make up your personal decision-making team.

The next chapter will introduce you to the languages in which your inner compass communicates its messages.

Your Inner Compass Team

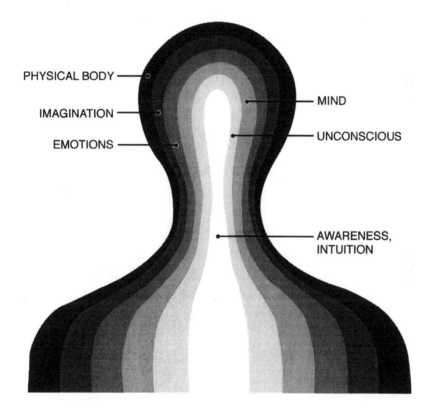

PHYSICAL BODY

IMAGINATION

EMOTIONS

MIND

UNCONSCIOUS

AWARENESS,
INTUITION

CHART 1.1

MULTIPHASE DECISION

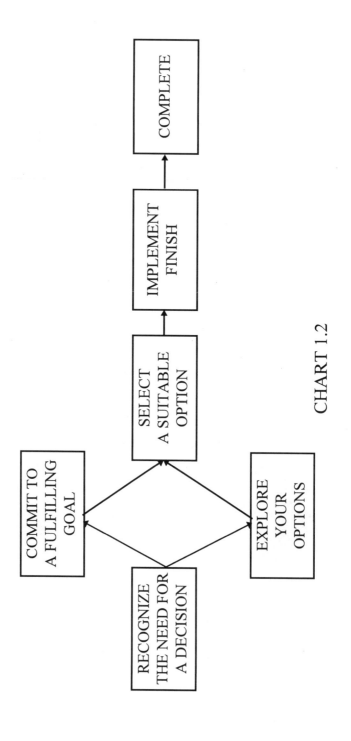

COMMIT TO
A FULFILLING
GOAL

RECOGNIZE
THE NEED FOR
A DECISION

SELECT
A SUITABLE
OPTION

EXPLORE
YOUR
OPTIONS

IMPLEMENT
FINISH

COMPLETE

CHART 1.2

2

Your Inner Compass Forecasts

This chapter will tell you how your inner compass communicates, what the Coach of your personal decision team is like and how your inner compass forecasts your decision outcomes.

The Languages of Your Inner Compass

Do you know that agonizing over a decision is like starving in the midst of plenty? Indeed, while you are making a decision, your inner compass is alive with messages to guide you and forecast your decision outcome. To "read" your inner compass you need to know its language. Each player encourages and warns you in its own language. Your Body speaks through its internal sensations and external mannerisms: through the way it breathes and moves, enjoys well-being or suffers. Your Imagination communicates through different images: auditory, gustatory, olfactory, visual, tactile. Your Emotions speak through various feelings – sadness and anger, compassion, and happiness, among others. Your Mind relates through words and numbers, thoughts and concepts. Your Unconscious clothes its messages in symbols (e.g., a crown is a symbol of power), while your Coach interacts through intuition -- an instantaneous knowing that depends on neither logical reasoning nor sensory information.

Each team member has a certain autonomy, a power over its own domain, and no one can replace any other. Words, the inhabitants of the mental domain, clearly cannot take the place of physical sensations like sniffing a flower or enjoying an orgasm. Indeed, words cannot even fully convey what these sensations are like. Similarly, your Emotions, however mighty, cannot produce a dinner. Unless your Body moves into action, you won't have food on the table.

Checks and balances in decision-making

In decisions, you cannot rely on just one player. Basing decisions only on your Mind's logic or only on your Emotions is like trying to appraise an art masterpiece with a ruler. The only thing you can learn from the ruler about a breathtaking piece of art is its size, since that is the only information the ruler can provide.

Each team member represents a major dimension of your environment. For instance, the Emotions inside of you pick up emotions outside of you. That is why you may feel depressed around depressed people and excited around people who are excited. When you become familiar with the language and character of a player on your decision-making team, the huge part of your environment this player represents opens to you and you benefit immensely from its decision-making clues.

The field on which you play your decision-making Game is a Land of Illusion and Change. To get a sense of its peculiarity, do the following simple experiment that takes about half a minute. Put a teaspoon into a glass with water and raise the glass until the surface of the water is level with your eyes. Do you see clearly that the spoon is broken at the water's surface? Take the spoon out -- it is intact. So much for "seeing is believing." You are dealing here with an optical illusion, based on the law of refraction. Optical illusions represent one of many kinds of illusions related to your Body. Your Body misleads you far more often than you realize.

If you have not already done it, take a minute now and perform the experiment described above to let all your players experience the illusions of the field on which you play your Game of Life, your decision-making. Not only your Body but all your players have a multitude of their own illusions. Sayings like "blind with rage" or "love is blind" refer to emotional illusions. Chapter 6 mentions numerous illusions to which your logical Mind succumbs. That is why, in the Land of Illusion and Change, if your Mind tells you something, it is wise to compare its message with clues from your Body, from your Emotions, and from your Unconscious.

> *To remain on the right track you need checks and balances that involve your entire decision-making team.*

Most likely, you have already realized that your team members were not chosen arbitrarily. Your Body represents the physical-material world, your Imagination – the astral realm, your Emotions – the causal realm, your Mind – the mental realm and your Unconscious – the etheric realm. While each player represents a major psychic realm, the Coach represents the first positive realm of Spirit.

Meet the coach of your personal decision team.

Given all those team members, it is natural to ask: Who am I? For an answer, let's turn to this famous exercise:

I have a Body, but I am not my Body.

I have Emotions, but I am not my Emotions.

33

Chapter 2

I have a Mind, but I am not my Mind. (1)

Apparently, there is a part of your being that observes all the players. We will call this quintessential part the "Coach." It is an ideal Coach, a wise and loving teacher who is always there for you. Whether you have performed beyond everyone's expectations or have just blown your best opportunity, if you turn to the Coach, the Coach gives you what you need most -- support, the courage to dare, a quiet understanding. To get in touch with the part of you that we call the "Coach," look at chart 2.1 at the end of this chapter . Take time to experience each face of your Coach, for instance, by re-living in your Imagination a situation when you experienced it, For example, re-live a situation when you experienced joy. Or, think of your kid, pet, song -- whoever or whatever triggers joy.

Awareness is life, and coaches are full of life. They love to participate in decision-making non-stop. Your Coach is after experience; your Coach thrives on experience. But your Coach's way of experiencing differs from your players' ways. The players are challenged mightily in the field -- the Body gets hurt; it gets addicted to food, sex, or drugs. Your Mind gets addicted to ideas and beliefs, your Emotions to relation-ships and roles, whereas your Coach remains unperturbed. A zestful participant but never a captive, your Coach is free.

Since your Coach can play the Game only through your players, each player is near and dear to the Coach's heart. All expressions of the players, even the wild and outlandish ones, are interesting, even fun to the Coach. Your Coach is not play-ing in the field, that is why the Land of Illusion and Change has no power over the Coach. While the players undergo dramatic changes -- your Body gets sick, your Emotions yo-yo up and down as euphoric and desperate thoughts come and go through your Mind, your Coach keeps its natural peaceful state, joyful and free. That guarantees your team's power to win the Game if your players follow the Coach's guidance.

But the Coach cannot impose guidance. Your players must turn to your Coach for it, and when they do, your Coach is always there for them to love, teach, inspire and share the knowledge of the bigger picture beyond the Game field. As your Coach aligns the players with freedom, joy, and peace, your Coach's awareness and energy flow into your players. What is it like to receive awareness and energy from the Coach? Maybe this story will provide a glimpse.

Soon after coming to the US, I had a medical emergency and surgery that left me unable to work. I had to go for treatments to a hospital where many patients were poor. I watched in disbelief as doctors slighted them, apparently assuming that the lack of money made these people ineligible for dignity. I myself was treated well until I developed complications. Not knowing how or unwilling to deal with them, the doctors chose to claim that I was healed. Never mind that I remained crippled and could not work. When I requested that I be referred to someone who could help, they reacted with rudeness.

My Emotions got upset. My Mind (as minds often do) pointed out the limitations of my situation -- the insurance for my treatment was already paid to this hospital; I had no money to pay someone else; without the treatment, I couldn't work. At that moment, I badly needed the support of my Coach. To connect with him I needed to detach myself from the drama of the situation. So in my Imagination I saw myself in a balloon lifting high in the sky. As I was soaring in its infinite vastness, concerns and limitations dropped away and I connected with the freedom of the Coach. My Mind, Emotions and my entire being filled with that freedom. At that moment I knew that there was no reason in the world for me to stay where I was. I thanked the doctors, walked away, and never came back.

35

Shortly afterwards, a friend recommended a doctor who brought me back to health.

The story had an unexpected sequel. Years later, as I was waiting for a speaker in a crowded auditorium at the University of Pennsylvania, a man knelt in front of me. He started begging for forgiveness. I asked, "Who are you?" He was shocked. "Don't you remember me? I am the doctor who treated you at that Medical Center. I knew you were in dire need of treatments and had no money to pay someone else. When you got up and walked away, I was shaken. I could not imagine anyone in your situation having that much freedom. I realized how badly I mistreated you. It became my nightmare, and it has haunted me ever since."

Clarity and strength appear when the team aligns with the Coach. But remember: the Coach cannot impose the guidance -- the players must turn to it.

Am "I" then the Coach? No, you are not. In decision-making, you are the team in its entirety -- the Coach, the players, and the relations bonding them all.

How to tune up your inner compass.

Harmonious relations within the team spell winning, while unbalanced ones erode connections with the Coach and push joy, freedom, and peace away. For instance, when the mind dominates, the decision-making team succumbs to "paralysis by analysis." When the emotions take over one's team, one behaves like a car on a steep icy slope, skidding down uncontrollably, the brakes and steering rendered useless. When the unconscious seizes control, one spaces out, gets drowsy, or otherwise loses touch with what is going on.

What harmonizes relations within your team? Focusing on any face of your Coach does. For instance, you can focus on observation. Start observing yourself, others and the entire scene, even when you're most disturbed. When you observe like a guest from another galaxy -- without doing anything, without demanding anything from yourself or others – you will most likely discover the humorous side of the situation. Humor can instantly harmonize and integrate the team.

Can You Trust Your Gut Feelings?

Where does the information that directs your decisions come from? Absolutely all of it comes from your team members: they are all you have to communicate with the world. Each move you make in decision -making, including an inner move -- a thought, an image, an emotion -- creates a response feeding information back to you on how your team and environment have responded. All feedback you receive comes from

⇒   your Body through its outer senses and inner sensations,
⇒   your Imagination through various images,
⇒   your Emotions through feelings,
⇒   your Mind through words and numbers,
⇒   your Unconscious through symbols,
⇒   your Coach through instantaneous knowing.

When feedback from your Body, Emotions, and Unconscious is strong, we call it "gut feelings." When it's not strong -- for instance, an almost imperceptible irritation -- we will call it "subtle clues."

Can you trust your gut feelings? Based on their experience, many people answer, "Yes." Take, for instance, Ray Kroc. In 1960 he asked the McDonald brothers to sell him their fast food franchise, including the name. The McDonalds set the price at $ 2.7 million, which at that time seemed unreasonably high. Kroc's lawyer strongly advised him against the deal. Kroc did not have that kind of money. Yet, his gut feelings kept urging him on. Kroc bought McDonalds and became a legendary success. Countless other cases suggest the importance of taking into account your gut feelings. Remember, however, that they come from your players who are affected by the Land of Illusion and Change. So their messages are sometimes clear and sometimes distorted. Each following chapter reveals more of how to "read" each player's messages and apply decision-making checks and balances with a high certainty of success.

Unlike your players, your Coach is free from illusions. So the messages of the Coach, expressed through awareness and intuition, come with exceptional clarity. That is a principal difference between feedback from your Coach and players.

Out of the vast pool of information that your players and Coach provide, only mental feedback expressed in words and numbers (verbal-numerical data) is commonly accepted in our culture as a legitimate basis for making decisions.

How credible are mental data?

It depends. Check it out. Charles in our next example did. While deciding what car to buy, he read consumer publications and talked with a dozen people who owned the model he liked. They were unanimously enthusiastic. So, ignoring his "gut" reservations, Charlie bought the car. It proved a major disappointment. What went wrong? To cut costs, the manufacturer had modified the model and Charlie happened to buy one of the first of these modified, inferior cars. In Charlie's case the most serious drawback of mental data came to the fore: *mental data reflect the past.* Now things change rapidly.

> *By the time you receive mental data,*
> *they are often outdated if not downright misleading.*

Of course, mental data are also misleading when they have been ineptly or fraudulently manipulated. But even if mental data come from a reliable source, how much sense does it make to project them into the future? How credible are the forecasts based on those data? Scientists usually answer in terms of probabilities and statistics. Are probabilities and statistics infallible? Not at all. Besides, they do not apply to the individual. For instance, statistical data can inform you that the IRS audits only 5% of the people in your area, but that does not tell you whether you will be part of that group.

How your inner compass forecasts.

What if you need a surgery and you are given these statistics. After this surgery, 95% of the patients fully recover but 5% get lethal complications. How do you know that it is not your lot to fall into the fatal 5%? That is where intuition, gut feelings and other nonverbal clues of your inner compass come to your rescue. By encouraging or warning you, they let you know how your personal decision team ranks your options. Nonverbal clues reflect not a statistical average but the interplay of all factors contributing to your situation at this moment.

> *Nonverbal clues express your decision-making uniqueness here and now. Their encouragement and warnings forecast outcomes of your decisions.*

Are nonverbal clues always credible? Can you trust them? It depends. Check them out. But do not ignore them -- they save lives. An example from the life of Beryl Markham, the first woman to cross the Atlantic in a solo flight, illustrates the point. In 1931-36 Beryl Markham flew passengers, mail, and supplies as a professional pilot in East Africa. With no radio and much of the terrain uncharted, the pilots had to rely on nonverbal clues. Once, a pilot named Woody failed to return from his trip. A two-day search for him turned up nothing. The next night, after delivering oxygen to a patient at 1 a.m., Beryl began her own search for Woody. By late afternoon she spotted his plane on the ground and managed to land her two-seater nearby, despite holes and rocks. Woody was nowhere in sight. Should she take off or continue searching? Woody had been missing for several days in a sun-parched place teeming with wild animals. She was unlikely to find him alive. Soon night would fall, and her runway would vanish in the darkness. Her fuel was low, and she struggled not to fall asleep. To make her decision, Beryl walked around Woody's plane, listening to its silence. She knew that in the silence, emanating from an object, the circumstance of its use lingers on. Here, even with night shadows flooding the earth, Beryl did not sense gloom. It was not the silence of death. So she continued her search for Woody. Soon she found him between two rocks, sick and unconscious from dehydration, but alive.

Some ridicule the use of subtle clues as "unscientific." But for centuries the now-highly-respected theory of probabilities was also ridiculed as "unscientific." World Wars I and II turned the tables. The growing complexity of war demanded drastic improvement in decision-making, and since probabilities and statistics help, they were accepted as legitimate tools. Now the time has come to legitimize nonverbal clues, and we should not need World War III to wake us up to that fact.

> *The central role in decision-making now belongs to nonverbal clues. Their encouragement or warnings communicate to you the wisdom of the moment.*

Wisdom of the moment.

What would you think of a driver who glanced at the road once and then kept driving based on what he saw when he started? Wouldn't you think he belonged in a mental institution? Yet often we go about decision-making the way he goes about driving. We stick to once chosen tactics and priorities although circumstances and environment rapidly change. Instant decisions succeed when they express the wisdom of the moment. To know it, pay attention to the nonverbal clues you are receiving. They deliver information pertinent to this moment. In a day or in five minutes the situation may change and so will nonverbal clues. My client Cliff shared an episode that illustrates the point. Before leaving a party, Cliff asked himself, "Is it time to hit the road?" Nonverbally, he got a "no." Ten minutes later, he asked again and got a "yes." (In the next chapter you will learn to get answers as quickly as Cliff did.) When Cliff hit the road, he saw a multi-vehicle accident. By starting ten minutes earlier, most likely, he would have been part of it.

In the next six chapters you will learn about various decision clues each member of your team issues and how to act on those clues. The rest is learned through practicing:

⇒ we recognize our clues,

⇒ we interpret them the best we can,

⇒ we trust our interpretation enough to act on it,

⇒ we evaluate the results, and …

⇒ we will do better next time.

It is a life-long adventure, full of empowering triumphs and opportunities to take advantage of the Accelerated Learning Device known as "Mistake." Fortunately, your inner compass team is available to you every day around the clock, and your Body, Emotions, Mind, and Unconscious virtually knock each other over in their eagerness to point out a right direction.

Summary

Pay close attention to nonverbal encouragement and warnings your inner compass issues. They forecast your decision outcome. Always apply decision-making checks and balances.

In the next chapter you will learn about instant clues from your Body that save lives and create fortunes.

AWARENESS

HUMOR

PEACE

JOY

PURITY

WISDOM

LOVING

FREEDOM

STRENGTH

YOUR
COACH

INTUITION

ALIVENESS

INTEGRITY

WONDERMENT

ENTHUSIASM

HARMONY

INSPIRATION

INTELLIGENCE

SUPERFLEXIBILITY

FULL PRESENCE

UNPREDICTABILITY

CHART 2.1

3

Instant Warnings
to Avoid Poor Decisions

In this chapter you will learn how the hidden wisdom of your Body can help you decide in seconds where it used to take hours, even days. You will also learn how your Body warns you – instantly! -- to avoid decisions that could worsen your health.

The First Player – Your Body

The first dimension of your inner compass is your Body. On your decision team, your Body is the only flesh-and-blood player. We tend to take it for granted since it is touchable with the hands, sizable with the eyes and seems so familiar. It is said that familiarity breeds contempt. But once you learn how your Body plays your Game of Life, never again will you take it for granted. Rather, you will treat it as the greatest wonder of the physical world. Indeed, it is.

How well do you use this wonder in your decision-making? Let us start with physical actions.

> ➤ What area in your life calls for change, i.e., troubles you (money, relationships, whatever)?
> ➤ Do you think about that area often?
> ➤ Do you often get upset about it?
> ➤ Do you take all the necessary actions ?

Remind yourself that your Body is *the only* player on your team capable of producing physical-material results. Wherever you want physical results, you must bring your Body into play.

> ➤ What simple action, like sending an e-mail or making a phone call, will get you moving?
> ➤ You may want to stop reading and take that step now

Sensory clues that speed up decisions.

Would you like to benefit more from decision clues delivered by sight, sound, smell, taste, and touch? Let's learn from the people who got more clues from sound than most of us do.

Beryl Markham, the first aviator to cross the Atlantic in a solo flight from East to West, grew up in East Africa. At 17, she lived alone in a thatched hut near the stables where she trained racehorses for their owners. One evening Beryl was scribbling notes about her thoroughbreds, the door of her hut open to the dark African night. Suddenly, she heard the sound of naked feet walking toward her... To Beryl, the sound conveyed important clues: It had no stealth; it was the honest sound. That was all she needed to make a decision not to lift her pen from the paper, not to raise her head. She waited for a word, and it came -- a word of greeting. At her door was standing her childhood playmate (1).

My mother also used sound richly for daily decisions. Her sense of smell atrophied when she was a child. Later in life she lost her eyesight so entirely that she could not tell day from night. Deprived of sight and smell, she relied on sound. Once she was frying onions (with little help she cooked delicious meals). I yelled from another room, "Mom, the onions are burning!" Unperturbed, she replied, "They've browned nicely, but didn't burn." She proved right. Surprised, I asked, "How did you know?" Now she got surprised, "Don't you hear? When onions burn, their sound is drier."

A simple "Hello. How are you?" reveals to a sensitive ear whether the speaker is open or closed up, calm or nervous, along with volumes of other information. Ancient healers (Egyptian, Greek, and others) used to diagnose patients by the sound of their voice. That tradition is alive today. Adepts in Oriental medicine can make a decision about a patient's condition within 30 seconds of hearing his/her voice in person or over the telephone (2).

All our senses deliver vital decision clues. Look for the clues, hear, feel and taste them, smell them out. Even if your senses have been long underused, they may awaken rapidly.

SENSITIZE YOURSELF TO CLUES FROM SOUND

> ♦Next time you're listening to a voice (on your car radio or wherever), ask, What does this voice tell me about the one who's speaking?

> ♦Prompt yourself further with: What else does his or her voice reveal?

Warning: This Decision Can Weaken Your Health

Hidden wisdom of your body.

Do you know that your Body receives information not accessible to your Mind? I learned that shortly after I came to the US. In an awareness training we were instructed to watch how our bodies would react to criticisms. At first, I was finding the criticisms thrown at me amusing. Then a slang phrase that I did not know made my entire body twist in pain. After the training

47

ended, I asked what that slang meant. What a surprise! Had I known its meaning, it would have definitely "pushed my buttons." That experience revealed to me that the body communicates with the world through its own instant means, independent of the mind. Indeed, where my brilliant scientific mind needed an explanation from someone, my body responded instantly. It means the body has a powerful role to play in making decisions. I guess God set up that elegant experiment to deliver me, then a worshipper of the mind, out of ignorance. Ever since I have been benefiting from the body's wisdom and I've taught others to use it in decisions through the following technique.

> ➤ Pick a situation where you need to make a decision
> ➤ List the available options and put the list aside
> ➤ Relax by observing your breathing
> ➤ Become aware of how your Body feels by mentally scanning it from nose to toes. Note any discomfort – tension, aches. You do not need to change anything
> ➤ Now imagine one of the options, for instance, the first one on your list and while imagining, observe any change in your Body sensations.
> ➤ All in all, does your Body feel better or worse than it did before you imagined this option?

STOP! Did you only read the description and skipped the actual steps? If so, again -- AGAIN!-- you left your Body out of the play! Do yourself a big favor -- experience how your Body votes right now. Discover its vote through these simple steps: (1) list your options, (2) relax, (3) observe your Body's condition, and (4) note how the inner sensations of your Body change while you are imagining each option.

> *If your Body feels better while your Imagination is previewing an option, it means that your Body favors this option. If your Body feels worse, it is a "no" vote.*

In your daily decisions -- about a business partner or investment, a life-mate or new suit, a house to buy or place to vacation -- avoid the options that weaken your Body and go with those which increase your Body's well-being. Once you grasp how the technique works, it will take you literally a fraction of a second to find out how your Body votes on an option. If it takes you longer, most likely you have started thinking. In other words, your attention has shifted from your Body to your thoughts or feelings. That muddles the result. Instead of your Body's response to an option, you are now getting your Body's response to your thoughts or feelings.

> *When you are imagining an option, your Body responds quicker than your Mind.*

To catch your Body's response, focus on how your physical well-being changes. Focus on noticing as many changes in your Body's sensations as you can. That will give you additional decision-making clues, keep your Mind busy and prevent it from interfering while you are imagining an option.

This is a great technique. It takes only a moment, and it helps you avoid decisions that would worsen your health. Yes, honoring the votes of your Body does help you screen out unhealthy options. Research showed that the body does not fully differentiate between the real and the imagined (3). While your Imagination is implementing an option, your Body's condition changes in the same direction in which it will change if you physically implement this option. Of course, you don't want to select an option that will worsen your Body's condition!

Chapter 3

It is worth repeating: when you are making a decision, your Body votes instantly(!) on the options in question, supporting sound options and warning you against selecting unfortunate ones. Taking into account the body's votes saves lives, health, and fortunes. Yet, surprisingly few people know about that and fewer yet use their body votes in decisions.

Ways in which your body warns you against making poor decisions.

Your Body votes through many instant changes in its inner sensations. Your heartbeat may quicken or "stumble," eyesight may blur or clear, breathing may deepen or get more shallow. Your Body may feel colder or warmer, heavier or lighter. Aches and pains may appear or vanish. Parts of your Body may go numb or, conversely, respond with tingling. Here are some clues my clients have noticed:

K: My frequent warning is pain in my left eye.

J: For me, lightness around the solar plexus spells encouragement and heaviness in the solar plexus spells warning.

S: When my jaw tightens, it's a warning. If I forge ahead anyway, I get myself in trouble.

C: When my voice suddenly gets hoarse, I need to shut up at once and switch to a receptive mode. If I ignore this clue and keep talking, inevitably I either say something I wish I hadn't or I miss important decision clues.

M: When my body starts feeling boxed in, it's a warning. When I feel the space around me expanding, it's an encouragement.

D: When my neck and shoulders stiffen, it's a signal to take a closer look at what and how I'm doing.

Real-life decisions based on instant warnings.

Joe came to me with a dilemma: to expand or not to expand his business. At the time he owned two trucks selling produce on the streets of Philadelphia and was offered the chance to put out three more trucks with no money down. Joe profited from his two trucks, but not without headaches. In bad weather few people bought from the trucks and produce perished. In the summer, some residents demanded that Joe remove his trucks because they attracted wasps and flies. With his third baby on the way, Joe badly needed money but was afraid to take the risk. We checked his body's votes. As Joe was imagining that he'd pass up the opportunity, his leg muscles tightened and his feet became as heavy as lead. As he imagined adding new trucks, his whole body felt light and energized. Joe did put out more trucks. As a result, he easily met increased family expenses and two years later became the proud owner of a nice produce store.

Dylon, a sophomore in college, had a different dilemma. For the first time in his life, Dylon had friends. Afraid to lose them, he kept up with their hiking, biking and parties. The trouble was that he had fallen behind in his studies. Could he party with his friends for a while longer? To find out, Dylon imagined doing that. His body responded with a headache. When he imagined that he buckled down and got on with his studies, his headache cleared.

George Soros is a financial genius. Over 26 years the investment fund he managed earned his shareholders an average annual return of 35%.(He is also a philanthropist, spending hundreds of millions of dollars to promote an open society in 25 countries, including South Africa and Russia.) In his book he reveals that when he himself was running his investment funds, he'd use his body feedback -- the onset of acute back pain -- as a signal that something was wrong in his portfolio. That signal would prompt him to look for what was amiss and to correct his strategies.

Warnings Particular to You

To find out how your own Body encourages and warns you in decisions start observing how your Body responds to various options. When watching your Body responses, make sure to pay attention to these three areas: muscle tension/relaxation, breathing, and energy level. Let us start with muscle tension/relaxation.

Tension and numbness in the body signal a lack of awareness. K. Stanislavsky, a famous Russian theater director, used to impress his students with this demonstration. He'd ask several strong students to lift and relocate a concert piano. While they carried the piano, he'd ask them a question from the multiplication tables. Each time the students would instinctively stop, put the piano down and only then answer. Indeed, the body's tension impairs even our ability to recall the multiplication tables, let alone make decisions. Like a badly twisted rubber hose impairs the flow of water, so does the body's tightness inhibit the free flow of the body's fluids and energy, causing us to miss vital feedback and perceive the world in a twisted way. That is why, *if the body tenses up while the imagination is previewing an option, it is a vote against the option.* The more your Body relaxes the more aware you are. Deep relaxation sets the stage for top performance.

What relaxes you? Supportive attitudes do. Observe how your muscles relax when you adopt the attitude, "the Universe supports me." Note how your muscles tighten when you judge - - yourself or others. In decisions, uptightness is a memo from your Body that reads, "Change your attitude in a hurry." Observe what images relax your Body. Do you relax when you identify with the sky? Does the smell of home-baked bread evoke calm in you? Can those images relax you in a jiffy before a stage performance or an interview?

The body relaxes when the mind focuses on breathing -- on the air as it goes in and out of the nostrils, on the diaphragm as it arches and flattens rhythmically, or on any other movement related to breathing. Right now take one minute to observe your breathing until your Body relaxes. If you find your attention has wandered away, simply focus back on how your Body breathes in and breathes out.

Languages reflect an intimate tie between decision-making and breathing. To "in-spir-e" means to bring in air and bring in spirit. Curiously, the Russian counterpart of "inspire" -- "vdykhat'" -- has the same structure. "V" is a prefix that means"in", "dykh" is the old Slavic for "spirit." A sheer coincidence? Inspiration comes with in-spir-ing, inhaling.

Do you want to make inspired choices? Then, before making a choice, take a moment to observe how your Body breathes in and breathes out. Then, if needed, take action. Focusing on your breathing increases your clarity and ability to know and do the right thing (4-6). When you feel overwhelmed or confused, first, observe your breathing, then hold your breath between inhalation and exhalation. That stabilizes the mind, helping it focus on a single point, for instance, on the question: What options do I have here?

To FIND OUT WHICH OPTION IS RIGHT FOR YOU:

> relax by observing your breathing
> imagine acting on one of your options and pay attention to how the imagining alters your breathing

Your Body favors options that make it easier to breathe, that improve the quality of its breathing.

(See exercises at the end of this chapter).

Your Body also favors the options that increase its energy and vitality.

Chapter 3

<u>WILL YOUR DECISION INCREASE YOUR VITALITY?</u>

> ➤ List options for a current decision you need to make and put the list aside
> ➤ Become aware of your energy level, i.e., how tired or energetic you feel
> ➤ While imagining one of your options, pay attention whether it makes you more tired or more energetic
> ➤ Continue this process for other options one by one
> ➤ Which option increases your Body vitality most?

The following exercise is designed to help you notice changes in the inner sensations <u>particular to your Body</u>. Similar changes occur when you make decisions.

<u>DISCOVER BODY FEEDBACK PARTICULAR TO YOU</u>

> ➤ Relax by observing your breathing
> ➤ Become aware of how your Body feels (scan it from your feet to the top of your head)
> ➤ Let your Imagination see, hear, and feel a person that disturbs you. How has your Body responded?
> ➤ Dismiss that from your Imagination
> ➤ Again relax by watching your breathing
> ➤ Let your Imagination see, hear, feel your favorite person and observe Body changes this imagining causes
> ➤ Relax by observing your breathing
> ➤ Think of an unpleasant situation. How has your Body responded to that thought?
> ➤ Think of your successful past decision. Let your Imagination see, hear, feel yourself after you have made and implemented it. How has your Body responded?

If after this exercise you notice no changes in your Body while imagining various options, turn to the exercises at the end of this chapter.

Your Body Delivers Sophisticated Decision-Making Information.

Your Body offers you much more than simple "yes" or "no" votes. Its clues carry sophisticated decision-making guidance. Here is a report from my client Leland, an executive at a Fortune 500 corporation. "Strangely, the option I thought of as the most attractive, where I was to work with the president of the corporation, produced a funny feeling in the pit of my stomach. At first, I identified it as anxiety, but it was more than that. It was a fear of trapping myself. I didn't know where it was coming from, but resolved to check it out. I discovered that the president's talk about my working for him was just lip service. He never committed to making it happen. And I was going to put my entire career on the line, counting on his full support! Body feedback spared me from walking off the cliff."

How does one find interpretations of his/her body feedback? Let's trace how Leland found his interpretation. First, he quietly observed the "funny feeling" in his stomach -- with the intention to get its meaning and use it in his decision-making. Tentatively, he labeled what he observed "anxiety." But he felt his label was neither accurate nor revealing enough. So, he kept imagining the option of working with the president and listening to his body responses until he realized that what he felt was a "fear of being trapped." Then he moved into action to check whether his interpretation was valid.

<u>TO INTERPRET YOUR BODY FEEDBACK:</u>

> ➤ Set an intent to get the meaning of your Body feedback and to use it in your decision
> ➤ Imagine acting on an option and observe your Body response
> ➤ Guess what it means

> ➢ Does your guess feel right? If not, keep imagining an option and observing all responses of your Body until you have another guess
> ➢ When your guess feels right, check it out

Often, when you hit the right interpretation and act on it, the signal vanishes, confirming that you got the message.

If a Body signal frequents you, take time to interpret it. Loretta, a teacher in a Child Care Center, noticed this signal—she'd rub her eyes with the back of her hands as children do. I suggested that for a week she jot down in which situations the signal occurred. At the end of the week, she discovered that she rubbed her eyes when she was around her boss of whom she was afraid, around the parents whom she perceived as intimidating and around her teenage daughter who has lately become rude and aggressive. Loretta commented, "What a childish thing to do!" That comment made her realize that she rubbed her eyes when she felt scared, as if saying to others and herself, "Don't demand more of me. I'm just a helpless child." Loretta, resolved to stop feeling intimidated. The next time her boss acted unfriendly and Loretta was about to rub her eyes, she asked instead, "Are you upset with me?' "Not at all," her boss replied. "It's the pain in my stomach that gets me."

INTERPRET YOU BODY'S SIGNALS THAT OCCUR FREQUENTLY

> ➢ Choose a signal your Body issues often
> ➢ Observe under which circumstances it occurs
> ➢ Jot down your observations, along with comments or guesses that might pop up
> ➢ Compare your observations. Let a common thread or pattern reveal itself

Example: I used to suffer from severe migraines. Observation revealed a clear pattern – my migraines would occur when I was running too many projects simultaneously. That pointed a way out. When I felt a migraine approaching, I'd ask myself which project was putting most pressure on me and I'd ruthlessly drop it. That ended my migraines. Of course, for someone else the cause of migraines might be entirely different.

Language comes in handy in interpreting body signals. For instance, "stiff-necked" means "stubborn." If your neck gets stiff, it is likely that you've been approaching a decision in a rigid way, and your Body tells you, "Get off your rigid position. Be flexible. Find a new approach." If you keep ignoring your Body feedback, you develop diseases. You can find interpretations of many body messages in books by L. Hayes(7.) Whether you agree with them or not, looking through them can help you interpret your own Body feedback.

As was mentioned in chapter 2, when the body 's responses are particularly strong, we call them "gut feelings." Emily Dickinson had a gut feel for poetry. "If I feel physically as if the top of my head were taken off, I know that is poetry." (8) In addition to gut feelings, the body sends out its messages via its subtle clues. When we cooperate with the body, i.e., take into account its feedback while making decisions, the body rewards us with more valuable information, helping us make instant decisions. Our sensitivity to body signals increases. Clues that yesterday were too subtle for us to notice, we perceive now as loud and clear. We begin to notice new kinds of subtle clues that used to be below our level of awareness. At such times, we appreciate anew our body and our progress. But if we disregard the decision-making input of the body, it will put less and less energy into its clues, and we won't perceive them at all.

These exercises increase sensitivity to your Body's clues.

Chapter 3

SENSITIZE YOURSELF TO YOUR BODY FEEDBACK IN DECISIONS

To Get More in Touch with Your Breathing: View the entire Body as one breathing organ. Remember breathing is effortless. If you feel "efforting," release your breath

> ➢ Imagine inhaling through the top of your head and exhaling through your feet
> ➢ Imagine inhaling from the bottom of your spine and exhaling through the top of your head
> ➢ Let your Imagination use the air to bathe your bones, muscles, organs; let the air wash out debris

To Increase Your Sensitivity to Tension and Relaxation

> ➢ watch the difference in your Body sensations as you flex and relax your toes, ankles, calves, thighs, the muscles of your stomach, abdomen, chest, lower back, upper back, then middle back
> ➢ Now tighten and relax your hands, arms, shoulders, neck, cheeks, muscles around the mouth

Journal Writing

> ➢ List in your journal specific Body responses you observe in each exercise
> ➢ Mark new signals you were not aware of before
> ➢ Daily write how you used Body signals in decisions
> ➢ Appreciate your progress

Summary

To speed up decisions, take into account how your Body votes. Choose decisions that get an instant "yes" vote from your Body – they will increase your Body's well-being.

⸺⸺⸺⸺⸺

In the next chapter you will meet your Imagination -- a player on your team who is chock full of magic.

4

Your Window into the Future

In this chapter, you will discover the astounding impact of your Imagination on decisions. You'll learn to use your Imagination as your window into the future through which you can shape your future more to your liking.

The Second Player -- Your Imagination

Your Imagination is your creative force. You activate it each time you imagine anything – scenes, tastes, smells, textures, sounds, feelings. Look at the chart at the end of this chapter. It lists unique character traits of your Imagination.

Each trait of your Imagination offers a thousand ways to speed up your decision-making.

First of all, your Imagination is free and so are you in it. Create anything you wish. Be, do, acquire whatever your heart desires. Freely receive and give love. Or luxuriate in doing nothing at all. Drink of ever-expanding freedom and ease. Nothing restricts you. *Limits and rules do not exist in the Imagination, unless, of course, you choose to create them.* Your Imagination is your Land of Fantasy. Here you can win debates with intellectual giants, enjoy outlandish adventures, whimsical sex, and if you wish, pain. Your Mind labels some fantasies "good", other ones "bad." Your Imagination, however, does not discriminate -- it just creates images of whatever you think and feel -- be it horror or pleasure. In your Land of Fantasy everything is effortless. If it isn't, it means you chose to create strain. "Undo" it – the strain vanishes.

Take a moment to come up with your most outrageous fantasy. Now unbridle your Imagination and watch it create even a more outrageous one in no time.

No matter what mood you are in, your Imagination can amuse and entertain you royally. Do you want to own an eight-mile-tall high-rise? Or would you rather turn moonlight into music? Your Imagination can grant you both. How about a private tour through and beyond (!) Creation with God Himself as your guide?

What Your Window into the Future Is Like

> *Your Imagination is designed to serve as your window into the future because your Imagination is time-free.*

While your time-bound Mind always functions in the past, present or future, in your Imagination time does not exist, unless, of course, you imagine it. (If you do, you can assign time any features you wish. What would your time be like?) Unlike your Body and Mind, *your Imagination is free from the tyranny of time*. Indeed, in your Imagination, you can be in the BC era or in the 25th century as freely as you are in the present. While your Mind needs time to accept new ideas and accept change, in your Imagination any change occurs at once. While your Body ages with time, your Imagination is ageless. While cells and systems of your Body need time to adjust their ways, in your Imagination any adjustment happens now, for in your Imagination the entire line of time -- the past, present, and future-- is available right now.

Since in your Imagination everything appears right now, it can serve as your window into the future. We have already used it as such in the previous chapter. Let's do it again now. Imagine implementing your current decision and watch -- right now -- how this decision will affect your Body in the future. You can do that because your Imagination is time-free and because your Body responds to the imagined like it does to a physical occurrence (more on that later in this chapter).

The time-free feature of the imagination also helps make instant decisions.

Your "Window" Helps Make Instant Decisions

What instant decisions have impressed you? Here are two that stand out in my memory. On the main street of Moscow (Russia), where I lived, a tall building was under renovation, scores of construction people working on the scaffolding. One summer day the street was crowded as usual. Suddenly, the scaffolding leaned toward one side and collapsed, burying construction workers and pedestrians. Only one man, a painter, escaped. When his place on the collapsing scaffolding became level with a window, he shattered the window glass with his paint bucket and jumped into the building, into safety. This painter knew the same secret as the driver in the next example.

His car hood flew open at 70 mph. The driver steered to a safe stop by shifting his eyes instantly to the road alongside of his door. How did he avoid the fatality that usually occurs in such cases? In the first fraction of a second, how did he know not to look ahead, not to do the panicky braking and steering that would kill? An industrial salesman who spent half his life on the road, he had played out in his imagination the handling of various road emergencies. In an interview he said that years in advance he had anticipated this particular emergency, and prepared to handle it (6.) So had the Moscow painter who jumped from the collapsing scaffolding. The thought that someday the scaffolding might collapse had crossed his mind many times, and in his Imagination he rehearsed many escape scenarios.

> *This is a secret of many successful instant decisions. In your Imagination rehearse in advance the handling of different scenarios of an upcoming challenge until you do it to your full satisfaction.*

Also, input from those who met similar challenges may help.

<u>Prepare for Making Instant Decisions in Emergencies</u>

> ➤ In what area of your life is an emergency most likely to show up?
> ➤ In your Imagination rehearse the handling of that emergency until you do it well
> ➤ While you still have time, take action to a/ prevent the emergency, b/ prepare to handle it well if it occurs

The Nobel prize winning use of the "window."
Joshua Lederberg won a Nobel prize for his decisions on the genetics of bacteria. He arrived at those decisions by imagining himself to be a chemical unit inside a bacterial chromosome. Another scientist, a chemist, identified so fully with the

molecules he was exploring that if the atoms in their proposed models were positioned too close to each other, he felt as uncomfortable as if his shoes were pinching (1). Those brilliant people received paramount decision-making information from their imagination.

How can you acquire that skill? By mastering the use of both the identifying and the space-free traits of your Imagination. "Space-free" means that your Imagination can go anywhere and take any space, shape or form. Unlike your Body, which is limited to its form and place, your Imagination can fit inside of the tiniest virus as effortlessly as it can encompass galaxies, zillions of light years away from each other.

DEVELOP THE SPACE-FREE FEATURE OF YOUR IMAGINATION

> ➤ Place yourself, first, inside a body cell, then into a microbe, and then into the nucleus of a hydrogen atom. What do you see, hear and feel there?
> ➤ Visit the North Star. What are you experiencing there?

When identifying with someone or something, pay attention to the difference between *making* imagery appear and *letting* it appear, i.e., between creating imagery and letting your Imagination present whatever it would. Those are two different modes of communicating with your Imagination. Sometimes both are simultaneously present, but if you pay attention, you will know which is which.

DEVELOP THE IDENTIFYING TRAIT OF YOUR IMAGINATION

> ➤ Choose any object around you -- a desk , a traffic light, a cloud, whatever -- and in your Imagination become that object. How would you experience life if you were, indeed, that object?

If you chose to identify with a cloud, it may go like this. You are a white cloud, weightless and free, in the sky above the beach. The wind is carrying you. Birds fly through you, causing a sensual feeling... Take time to identify more fully. At first, like a baby, you are aware only of yourself. Gradually, you begin to relate to your environment – to the blue sky above you, the ocean beneath, other clouds approaching to merge...

> ➢ Identify with the key person(s) in your current decision
> ➢ Experience your decision from their perspective
> ➢ How can you now ease and speed up your decision?
> ➢ Now identify with the success of your current decision
>   How can you speed up from that perspective?
> ➢ What insights have you gotten?

For example, my client Tom decided to raise a million dollars to modernize his business equipment. I suggested that he identify with this money. So in his imagination he became a million dollars in $100 bills, 10,000 of them. Then he let his imagination show him whatever it would. (Note: in his imagination, he is not Tom now – he is the money.) The bills began flying to Tom and clinging to his chest and belly. Tom grabbed them and threw away from his body in disgust. That revealed that Tom still viewed money as filthy. After that attitude was cleared, Tom was able to find an investor.

TO INCREASE YOUR ABILITY TO RECEIVE MONEY:

In your Imagination:

> ➢ Go to a comfortable place. Make yourself comfortable.
> ➢ Let the desirable amount appear -- in cash – near you.
> ➢ Switch roles -- become that money. Observe what happens. Experience yourself as money would. From the

money's perspective, what are you like and how can you open yourself to receive more?

➢ What do you presently need to decide upon? Identify with him/her or it and start experiencing life from that perspective.

Don't ask, "How do I do it?" In the Land of Fantasy you can do, be, and have anything.

> _Repeatedly_ identify with what you want to become, experience, or receive and _each time_ jot down insights you gain from the identification.

Keep experiencing life from the perspective of who or what you're deciding upon and you may find breathtaking options for your current decision.

Your "window" is a zillion times more powerful than TV.

Your Imagination influences profoundly your entire decision team, starting with the Body. Imagine right now that you are lifting heavy weights. Or, imagine: you are testifying in front of a hostile committee. Your Body reacts with sweating, blood pressure goes up, brain waves change. Note: you were only imagining. _Laboratory tests confirm that fantasies bring forth significant biochemical, neurological, electromagnetic, and other changes._ That is why your Body, including its immune system, responds with healing to images of health and with disease to imagined illnesses (3, 4).

Do your Emotions respond to your Imagination? You bet! Your Emotions go up or down with imagined scenes as they do with non-imagined ones. For instance, when you imagine that someone rejects you, your Emotions get as upset as if the rejection had actually occurred. What images frequent you? Pay attention, because your Unconscious treats persisting imagery

65

as a project to implement, as a goal to win. Do you constantly hold images of food? Your Unconscious will surely draw you to those foods. Replace the food images with the images of your success, and the Unconscious will draw you to success. Like your Imagination, your Unconscious does not discriminate. If you dwell on failures, it brings you failures. If you dwell on great goals, it draws you to those goals. That is why, sages teach, "Always win in your fantasies!" Since your Imagination is *your* Land of Fantasy, if you don't like something here, change it. If your spouse, child or boss do not treat you royally in your fantasy, kick 'em out: it is *your* fantasy!

At your own volition, imagine only what you want – health, happiness, peace. If an image of someone, who, for instance, mistreated you pops up, reverse it. Imagine that person speaking about you at a large gathering in the most glowing terms.

Unlike other players, your Mind attempts to clearly distinguish imagined events from those taking place physically. But later on, the Mind forgets which is which.

You noticed, of course, that even a momentary exposure to a TV program can leave a profound trace.

> *Your Imagination is your inner TV, a zillion times more powerful than the TV box in your room.*

Not only do all your team members see and hear every program your Imagination runs, they also smell, feel, and taste its programs 24 hours a day, day after day, all your life long. Do you realize what an impact it has, what a tremendous power your Imagination wields??

Those who dismiss the Imagination as "just fantasy" are ignorant of its true power and of the magic the Imagination brings to decisions. Actively use your Imagination as your window into the future. Examples below show that the pay-off is stunning and inspiring.

Nicola Tesla, a genius whose inventions changed the world of our technology, developed his inventions in his imagination, without touching anything physically until the final stage. He imagined turbines, generators and other machines so graphically that when something was out of balance in them, he would notice and correct it *in his imagination*. When Tesla put his final product to the test physically, it worked exactly as he had planned it. "In twenty years there has not been a single exception" (2). Can you imagine how much time and money Tesla saved by testing his inventions in his imagination?

In his autobiography, Tesla describes how he developed the powers of his Imagination. To take his mind off an affliction he suffered in his childhood, Tesla started journeying in his Imagination beyond his small native town in Croatia. At first, the new scenes were blurred. When he tried to concentrate on them, they vanish. But by and by the scenes grew more distinct until, finally, they gained the concreteness of real things. He journeyed every night and sometimes during the day to new places, cities, and countries. He'd live there, meet people and make friendships that became as dear and intense for him as those in his physical life. He practiced that until, at the age of 17, he became interested in inventions. To his delight, Tesla discovered that he needed none of the physical props other inventors used. He could finish his inventions in his Imagination.

Tesla observed that when one rushes to implement a crude idea physically, unavoidably, material details and defects dissipate the power of his concentration. That is why he maintained that implementing an idea in the imagination was a superior way to materialize ideas. Harnessing the power of the imagination helped Tesla become one of the greatest and most fertile inventors of the 20th century.

<u>USE YOUR IMAGINATION IN EACH DECISION-MAKING PHASE</u>

> ➢ In your journal, list at least ten ways to speed up each phase of multiphase decisions through your Imagination
> ➢ Keep adding to the list as you read the rest of the book
> ➢ Enrich your list by reading, for instance, (9)

Enjoy the Fruits of Your Future Success Now

How to use your "window" to shape your future

To shape your future to your liking you must, first of all, shape your self-image to your liking. Your decision-making depends heavily on your self-image -- on how you stereotyped yourself in your Imagination. When your Imagination portrays you as a certain type of person, you move, feel, think, behave and even smell exactly like that type of a person. Your players respond to life according to the stereotype of you that your Imagination holds. That is why no matter what great outer goals you have achieved, *your life will not improve unless you have upgraded your self-image.* Here is a classic example. Years ago, a renowned plastic surgeon removed a big ugly hump in the nose of a British duchess. Her face became one of classic beauty. But instead of enjoying a new life, she kept on living as an unwanted ugly duckling (5). Why? She failed to upgrade her self-image.

> *Each goal has two sides -- the inner and the outer. The outer is the tangible physical result you are after (e.g., a house, degree, supportive relationship financial independence.). The inner goal is the upgrading of your self-image.*

Most people assume that if they achieve their outer goal, their self-image will automatically adjust to where it needs to be.

Not necessarily! Most often, it does not. This parable shows what happens.

A farmer works in his fields from dawn to dusk. In the fall he celebrates a rich harvest. Only he didn't take time to build a silo for his crops. He rushes to build one. Too late. His rich harvest perishes under heavy rains, strong winds, and early snow.

Winning the outer goal brings with it new challenges: fans' adoration, scrutiny by professional fault-finders, new financial responsibilities, an avalanche of opportunities. If your players are still tied up with "building the silo," new challenges knock you down. That is what we see time after time with new sports and movie stars. Overnight success evaporates overnight unless you have already firmly upgraded your self-image, especially its vital component – self-trust. Here is a graphic example of how gradually ever higher levels of self-trust develop.

If a doctor wants to become a surgeon -- after medical school -- he puts another five to seven years into learning his trade. A moderately adept MD certainly does not need that much time to learn the "mechanics" of surgery -- how to cut, sew, and tie knots. What, then, takes so long? The acquiring of surgical decision-making skill does. It is the skill to make instant decisions that minimize risks for each patient. This skill builds bit by bit through endless hours of service. The spark that ignites decision-making power is self-trust (not to be confused with smugness). As the surgeon sweats blood over punctured lungs and inflamed gall-bladders, as he learns to handle a host of unanticipated problems, like the sudden gushing of blood from a vessel, he upgrades his self-image. He comes to perceive himself as the one upon whom he can rely. In the sea of uncertainties that is so much a part of surgery, it is easy to doubt himself, especially after his mistake has contributed to a patient's death. But he learns to survive the inevitable errors and become a better surgeon with each case. Those who succumb to doubts leave. They have to. Because once a surgeon is in practice for himself, solely responsible for the human life pulsating in his hands, he needs self-trust like air.

Inner and outer goals are not equal in value. The inner goal carries more weight, because if you failed to upgrade your self-image, no outer achievement can truly deepen your joy, freedom, and peace.

Take Carl, for instance. He works with emotionally disturbed people and shares a house with a tumultuous couple. His inner goal is to find peace. His outer goal is to rent an apartment in a quiet neighborhood. But however quiet the apartment, it won't help if he fails to win his inner goal.

But once in your Imagination, you have experienced the new you over and over, you have created an inner *magnet*. Each time you feel, see, hear, and smell the new you physically or in your Imagination, the inner magnet pulls to you the outer goal that resonates with your new self-image.

If you have your self-image upgraded, you are already a success. With a new self-image, you may not even need that outer goal you were shooting for, and if you do, it will be easier to reach it. Upgrading your self-image is your insurance against failure. There is an important dynamic between the inner and outer goals. Pursuing the outer goal brings forward the experiences you need in order to develop and anchor your new self-image. In other words, after you have set up your inner goal, pursuing an outer goal helps you achieve the inner one.

To enjoy the fruits of your future success now hold a rapt vision of your goal.

⇒ *Without a clear vision you will inevitably get sidetracked.* The clearer the vision, the faster you win.

⇒ The time invested in creating a clear vision is as vital for you as the time of pregnancy is vital for the baby and the mother-to-be. It is the time that prepares the creator (you) and your creation (your goal) for the new life. While your Imagination is holding your vision of a goal, an invisible but vital change occurs. Each player – your Body, Emotions, Mind and Unconscious – adjusts to winning this goal. That is why, each preview of your goal in the Imagination accelerates your decision-making tremendously. During previews: a/ each player inches, leaps, propels toward the goal and b/ you discover delightful shortcuts that eliminate waste.

⇒ A splendid vision helps you win a splendid goal. While creating a vision, go for the very best. In the Land of Fantasy, all God's riches are at your disposal -- the most vibrant colors, the purest sounds and sublime qualities. It is your magic time to take freely from the smorgasbord of the Universe. Take, however, only what you can put to good use.

⇒ Unlike the escape-from-reality fantasies, the vision happily marries artistic freedom and businesslike thrust, producing the seed from which your creation -- your goal -- grows. As the seed draws from the soil all the nutrients it needs to develop into a plant, so does your vision draw to you all the resources you need to win the goal. The vision broadcasts to the Universe your readiness to win your goal, and you may receive more assistance than you ever dreamed possible.

It was his splendid vision that turned a shy man, known to few Parisians, into the king of world fashion. His name was Christian Dior. When asked to revamp an ordinary design shop, Dior proposed instead to create a high-fashion enterprise under his name. In 1946, amidst all-masculine wartime fashion with its square shoulders and platform shoes, Dior suggested an utterly feminine look of simple elegance. A textile tycoon, Boussac, backed Dior with money at once. Why? Such was the splendor and precision of Dior's vision that Boussac simply

71

knew that Dior was bound to succeed (6). Indeed, from his sensational success in 1947 until his death ten years later, Christian Dior indisputably reigned over the world of fashion.

⇒ *People who regularly find rapture in their vision triumph.* Here is an impressive example. A sixty-one-year-old patient was written off by his doctors as incurable. His throat cancer made it hard for him to breathe; he could barely swallow his own saliva, and his weight had dropped to that of a child. Fortunately, he was introduced to healing imagery and instructed to play with it for 5-15 minutes, three times daily. He embraced the program wholeheartedly, giving each experience his rapt attention. In two months he showed no signs of cancer (3). Thousands of other "incurables" owe their recovery to healing imagery (3,4).

When Arnold Schwarzenegger decided to become the # 1 body builder, *every night* before falling asleep he imagined himself a winner (7). Mary Lou Retton, the first American woman to win the Olympic gold in gymnastics, also practiced in the Land of Fantasy *daily* to perfect her sport routine and her emotional responses to Olympic challenges (8). So did Greg Louganis, who won four Olympic medals in diving.

All those people – *regularly* – luxuriated in imagining themselves being, doing, having what they truly wanted.

PAY FOR WHAT YOU WANT WITH ... MOMENTS OF RAPTURE

1. Write down your current outer goal --the tangible material result you want from your current decision-making round.

2. Imagine that you have won your outer goal. How do you feel about yourself after winning?

Let's say your outer goal is to form a fulfilling relationship. Assume that you've got the most loving, supportive, ... (fill in the blank) relationship. How do you feel about yourself? Confident? At peace? Adventurous? Whatever it is, play it out in your Imagination until the experience becomes concrete, alive, and strong inside of you.

If your outer goal is a new job, assume you've got it. How do you feel about yourself now that you have this job? What is the new you like? How do you treat yourself and others in a new way? How do you sit, walk, listen, do things, enjoy life? All in all, what is new in your experience of yourself?

If your outer goal is to acquire a certain amount of money, assume you've got that amount. What is the new you – having all this money – like? How do you experience yourself and your daily life in a new way?

3. Once you have a sense of your inner goal, i. e., of how you want to upgrade your self-image, it is time to claim it. As with insurance, claiming requires a certain procedure. First, describe the newness in yourself that you want and how it will show. Use the present tense, as if the newness is already yours.

Carl, whom you met in the previous section and who chose inner peace as his inner goal, began cultivating within himself stillness by imagining at certain times that he knew stillness. Soon, an acquaintance mentioned a man who was being relocated to Alaska and needed to sell his house promptly. Carl looked at the house, fell in love with it and chose as his outer goal to acquire the house. At that point, Carl described in his journal the newness in himself that he wanted, using the present tense, as if he had already achieved his goals. "Having bought this house, I feel peaceful. I don't run around anymore like a chicken without a head. I take time to chew my food, buy comfortable shoes, and listen to my favorite clarinetists. I listen to people without interrupting them, as now I have the peace to enjoy each person's rhythm. I feel in sync with life. At work, rather than reacting explosively to emotionally disturbed people, I retain my peace."

4. Now affirm in 6-12 words the essence of the newness you want. Finding an affirmation that resonates inside of you is like filing your claim with the insurance company.

Carl's affirmation: "I am using each person and each experience to deepen my peace."

5. Now the insurance company has to process the claim. In your case, the processing moves ahead each time your Imagination feasts on your desired inner experience.

Since Carl is after peace, he imagines that he *is* peace, listening, feeling, moving, eating, relating to everything and everyone as peace. He imagines every cell in his Body becoming tranquil and serene. The outer goal of the mentioned earlier cancer patient was healing. His inner goal -- the upgrading of his self-image -- was crucial to his healing. From his old self-image of a helpless man he moved to a new self-image of a man who wielded the power to change the course of his life.

For the upgraded self-image to take root, savor it regularly. Without that regularity the players regress.

> *The regularity and persistence of the imagery you entertain let your Unconscious know what to bring into existence.*

Winners know the value of regularity. In two months, the cancer patient was to imagine his goal 3 times a day for 61 days, i.e., 183 times. He missed only one time (3). Schwarzenegger never fell asleep without imagining himself a winner (!) (7)

6. To maintain the regularity of imagery, let your Imagination run a miniseries on your new self-image for 3-15 minutes at prime times -- when your subconscious is most receptive -- upon awakening and before retiring at night. As you repeatedly feast on your newness -- feel it inside, see it, hear it, sense it, smell it -- it keeps expanding, deepening, sparkling with new facets. Each time watch the miniseries until the

next step toward the newness or yet another of its facets appears. Luxuriate in this new facet or step.

After watching a miniseries on his new self-image for the first time, Carl reported, "I see myself walking from the parking lot to my office. I hear my friendly voice greeting people; I feel relaxed. Before entering the rooms where the emotionally disturbed people are, I surround myself with peaceful white light and send the light ahead of me, as I was taught long ago. In the rooms, people play the same roles I've seen them playing many times before. But today, instead of maddening me, the scene strikes me as funny. I feel calm and compassion."

7. Once you grasp a new step, new facet, or a new development toward desirable newness, anchor that by describing it briefly and specifically in your journal.

Carl jotted, "a/ I'm to remember to surround myself with and to send ahead of me white light. b/ Humor felt as an aspect of peace. "

8. To measure your progress, give yourself 5 points each time during the day when you feel and act as the new you. Do your best to score at least 10 points daily. Better yet: each day score 5 points more than the day before.

RECEIVE HEALING WHEN ANCHORING YOUR NEW SELF-IMAGE

- ➤ Each time you act as the new you, stop for a moment and appreciate yourself as success
- ➤ Note how your Body responds to genuine self-appreciation with healing
- ➤ Record in your journal which part of your Body received the appreciation (and healing) this time
- ➤ Or, do the self-appreciation at the end of each day as you recall the times when you acted as the new you

Carl: "As I appreciated myself for finding humor in what used to madden me, I felt warmth in the middle of my spine." It means Carl's spine has become more alive, hence, more able to communicate decision-making clues.

How long do you do those exercises? You do until you have integrated the desired newness into your self-image. Likewise, your insurance claim is kept in the outstanding file until it is awarded. More on the inner goal in chapter 10.

How to Get Free Advice from the Best

Usually, implementation of a decision requires new skills, new character qualities, new habits, new attitudes. It takes a long time to develop them, unless you turn to your Imagination. Remember: most of your team takes the imagined for real. So by imagining that you already have a desirable skill, you help your team respond to the world as if you really have it. In that way you claim your future skills now.

Your Imagination can also instantly put you in touch with the greatest people in any area of life where you seek success. For instance, do you need to prepare for a media interview? No problem. Let's invite Robin Williams. Once he appears, enjoy the spontaneity, humor, and ease that emanate from him in front of the cameras. Imagine that this emanation penetrates you, awakening your own spontaneity, warm humor and natural ease. Enjoy observing him until you feel relaxed and ready to exchange jokes with Robin. Do you want to have your tongue treated with an anti-blunder substance? Your Imagination can do that in no time. Anything else?

In your Land of Fantasy, get together with Masters as friends. Ask for their input. You may get excellent and, mind you, free advice. Then *practice, practice, and practice.*

> *Your Land of Fantasy is a great place to practice being right now what you want to become.*

Here is Andrew, who was so terrified of public speaking that he'd faint when called to say something in front of the class. Nobody could help until Andrew created an image of himself as a witty and charming speaker. He began to practice that role in his Imagination a few times daily. In his Imagination he invited Winston Churchill to coach him. Gradually, Andrew became able to speak freely to his class. Next, he ran on his inner TV a miniseries on himself communicating successfully with hostile crowds. As his performance in the Land of Fantasy improved, so did his outer performance. Andrew graduated into a much sought-after (and highly paid) speaker.

Summary:

If you don't use your "window," you're losing time, money & fun! Your Imagination is designed to serve as your window into the future. You absolutely owe it to yourself to take advantage of the speed and fun, ease and effectiveness your Imagination contributes to decisions.

> *It is your most pleasant responsibility to engage your Imagination each time you encounter a decision-making challenge.*

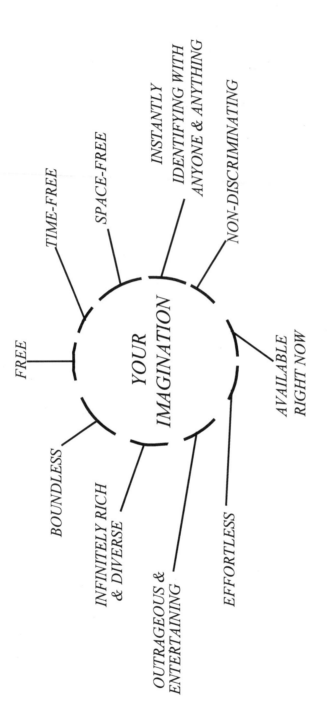

TIME-FREE

SPACE-FREE

INSTANTLY
IDENTIFYING WITH
ANYONE & ANYTHING

FREE

YOUR
IMAGINATION

NON-DISCRIMINATING

BOUNDLESS

INFINITELY RICH
& DIVERSE

OUTRAGEOUS &
ENTERTAINING

EFFORTLESS

AVAILABLE
RIGHT NOW

CHART 4.1

5

How to Use Emotions to Make Sound Decisions

This chapter explains what emotion is, how to avoid emotional traps and how to use your anger, frustration and other Emotions to produce sound decisions.

The Third Player – Your Emotions

Have you ever been flooded with emotions and made a decision you bitterly regretted later? Everyone has, even cool diplomats, great scientists and admired world leaders. That is why many people fear emotions in decisions. Yet, we cannot survive without emotions like we cannot survive without water.

Emotions are to decisions what water is to Earth.

Water creates floods, but we learn to harness its energy. Likewise, we can harness the energies of emotions so that they carry us over obstacles and help us navigate human interactions. For instance, if negative emotions keep flaring up over an issue, their message may be, "Your approach is not working. Change your approach." Here is a historical example.

Tension was palpable at the 1978 Camp David summit set up to negotiate peace between Egypt and Israel. Israeli Prime Minister Begin was tense because the issues in question had life-death implications for his country. Egyptian President Sadat was tense because of numerous death threats he received from those Arabs who were against peace in the Middle East. The long-standing animosity between the two nations permeated the atmosphere. Sadat and Begin either argued bitterly over old wounds or refused to meet. On the eleventh day the talks broke down, and Sadat was packing to leave. Then President Carter changed his approach. He took to Begin the pictures of the three leaders together autographed for Begin's grandchildren, each picture carrying the name of the grandchild to whom it would go. In his memoirs, President Carter recalls that when Begin noticed his granddaughter's name on the top picture, his lips trembled and tears welled up in his eyes. He shared with Carter a little about each of his grandchildren, especially about the one who seemed to be his favorite. Both leaders became emotional as they talked quietly about grandchildren and about war (1). Deep loving melted walls of separation, and Mr. Begin made an unheard of move. He went to Sadat's cabin, and they communicated beautifully. Soon, the peace agreement between Egypt and Israel was signed. Can, indeed, such personal moments turn around a conference of international significance? Absolutely. Our leaders are humans, and it is true of all humans that deep loving emotions unify people and inspire win-win decisions.

What is emotion, then, and how is it triggered? That is answered in the first part of this chapter. The second part addresses the harnessing of various emotions. Please note: In this chapter the term "emotions" encompasses emotions outside and inside us. When the word "Emotions" is capitalized, it refers to a player on your own decision team. To emphasize a subjective awareness of the emotions inside we use the term "feelings."

What is emotion?

Look at the various faces of emotions (charts 5.1 and 5.2 at the end of this chapter). Can you name the prevailing emotion for each picture? When you know which emotions you are dealing with, it is easier to harness them. What do all the emotions have in common?

The word "emotion" comes from the Latin "emovere," which means "to move out, stir up, agitate." All emotions -- positive and negative -- are specific, highly volatile energies which, by exciting or provoking, cause you to act. Your Emotions are your action-causing player in decisions.

In itself, no emotion, positive or negative, is bad or wrong. Whether you benefit from an emotion or let it trouble you is up to you. The value you receive from any emotion depends on how you use it.

Recognize your moments of power.

The moments when your Emotions surge, considerable energy becomes available to you. During such moments ordinary people perform deeds of heroism, like that mother who lifted a car to rescue from under it her child. But when emotions surge, ordinary people also kill others and themselves. The moments when emotions surge and peak are critical: you can either harness emotional energies and ride them toward your goal, or, they will ride you elsewhere -- usually, into deep trouble. If you can direct that surge of energy at your volition, these are your moments of power. Example from a workplace. Bob has just been hired as a sales manager for a computer company. As he is preparing his first presentation to the company's board of directors, a sudden thought, "They won't like me," makes his knees go weak from fear. This is Bob's moment of choice. He can either let fear discourage him or use the energy of fear to prepare such an enthusiastic presentation that he'll win over the board members. All of them!

By their nature, emotional energies are highly volatile and mercurial; they can run out of control and spread quicker than summer fires in dry forests. Some people think they cannot catch those moments of choice, let alone direct their emotions. I ask, "How do you feel when someone on a freeway cuts in front of you, a hair's breadth from an accident?" They say, "I get so angry I'm ready to kill 'em!" I ask, "Do you hit their car to let them know how you feel?" They say, "No." I ask, "What do you do?" They say, "I keep driving to my destination." If you do, it means you are able to manage emotions. To ease that task, you may want to find out more about your Emotions.

What triggers emotions?

1. Most emotions are triggered by thoughts. When upset, ask yourself, "What have I thought a moment ago?" Usually, you can trace your upset to what you thought just prior to it. Watch how Susan's feelings change following a dramatic change in her thoughts. On the phone with her friend Connie, Susan was crying, " Steve has left. I can't live without him…"

Gently, Connie reminded Susan of Steve's explosive anger and many occurrences that were far from rosy. Susan's thoughts changed to " Really, thank God, I don't need to deal any longer with his angers, depressions and dirty socks. Hey, I'm a free woman!" Her self-pity evaporated, yielding to a sense of relief and exhilaration. Most often our emotions do act as puppets of our thoughts. When we manage to laugh at ourselves, these puppet shows are fun to watch.

2. We pick up emotions from others. Walk into a classroom before an exam or into a courtroom and watch how the emotions of excitement and anxiety wash over you, although you are not part of that exam or litigation. We resonate with other people's emotions as though we have inside a radio receiver and transmitter with a particular frequency band corresponding to each emotion. When someone around us, say, gets angry, our anger band is activated. That resonance allows us to know what other people feel. Of course, the other side of the coin is that our own feelings broadcast to others what we feel even when we are silent. Can we protect ourselves from the emotions that float around? Yes, we can. Later in this chapter you will learn how.

3. We pick up emotions from things and places. Real estate agents observe that empty houses where people were happy retain warm emotions long after their owners left, while the houses where unhappiness lived retain unsettling emotions. Once you learn how emotions permeate your environment, you may want to keep around you the protective shield, described later in this chapter.

4. Emotions may be stirred by past hurts stored in your Unconscious. For instance, a symbol may trigger terror or

another powerful emotion, and you may have no clue why, since you have no corresponding conscious memory. The more you have your Unconscious cleaned from the excess baggage of the past, the less you will be affected by unconscious energies.

Emotions Deliver Information
and
Cause Action

In the open sea we pay close attention to navigating devices. In human relations, our navigating devices are feelings, and people who take them into account avoid lots of trouble. What are the signs of emotional feelings? The outer signs come up in speech when emotions despair, shriek, lament, triumph and otherwise create drama:

"She went with another guy! My life is *totally* ruined..."

"That dealer is *the meanest* crook on earth!"

"I'd *never* give that bastard a dime!"

"I have conquered the world!"

Emotions exalt or inflame one's speech with exaggerations and absolutisms, curse words and rude or dramatic phrases. Emotions transform the timbre of one's voice to its sweetest, or, conversely, turn up its volume, unrecognizably heighten its pitch, muddle its purity and render it hoarse.

Emotions also induce countless changes in bodily expression: eyes flare or fog up, faces turn pale or ruddy, the muscles around the mouth, shoulders and all over the body tighten. We may sweat and hold breath. The list goes on.

Being aware of the outer signs of emotions helps us avoid conflicts with people as we go about our decisions. We can time our interactions with people well if we trace how emotional energies move -- rise, climax and subside. If we do not, we are in for rough sledding, as Marilyn learned when she asked her neighbor Holly for a small favor. Holly refused so angrily that Marilyn barely suppressed tears. The next day Holly apologized. "Please, Marilyn, don't take it personally," she said. "I received some awful news right before you came up…" Then Marilyn recalled pink blotches on Holly's face -- the signs of Holly's highly emotional state. "How could I have done better?" asked Marilyn. Holly said, "When I get like that, just wait out until I calm down like you wait out a heavy rain."

Some people display no outer signs of emotions. Are they emotionless? Not at all. To detect their emotions you want to pay attention to the inner signs.

> *The inner signs of emotions are changes in your own feelings.*

DIFFERENTIATING YOUR FEELINGS FROM THOSE YOU HAVE PICKED UP FROM OTHERS

This differentiating requires awareness and uncompromising honesty with yourself. When you have that, here is how you can differentiate:

> ➤ Before interacting with others, become aware of your own Body and feelings
> ➤ If your feelings change, ask yourself, "Who or what here arouses my feelings? Which ones? Am I invested in the outcome?
> ➤ If the answer is "no," then changes in your feelings may mean that you picked up emotions from others

With practice, you get used to taking feelings into account the way you take into account traffic lights when driving. Then you come to appreciate feelings as excellent navigators.

Kate certainly does. An expert on workers' compensation, she lost her job to downsizing. Her adjustment to self-employment wasn't easy. Finally, she met a representative of a large corporation who was obviously impressed with her expertise. But he asked her to reduce her fee. Kate suggested that he take up the matter with his boss. The rep agreed. Yet, his feelings communicated strong discomfort, and Kate picked it up. His feelings told her, " I want to use your service, but if you refuse the fee I'm offering, I won't be able to. I'm scared of my boss." Kate got the message and agreed to his fee. Future events confirmed that she read the message correctly. How did she know that the uncomfortable feelings were his, not hers? In preparation for the meeting, Kate resolved that for such a prestigious client she'd be willing to start for a nominal fee. Also, she had a feeling that if this deal fell through, another one would soon come her way. So at the meeting her emotions were calm and she was free to observe the flow of the Game.

Recognizing the inner signs of emotional presence gives you a leading edge in business and other human interactions.

> *To get a sense whether people give you honest answers, observe whether their feelings match their words. Words disguise truth easily -- feelings do not.*

Here is an example from a workplace. Put in charge of an international trade show, Helen keeps a vigilant eye on deliveries from all over the world. Only a week is left before the opening, and she is checking on Bill who was to deliver special computer cables. He is swearing on his honor that the cables will arrive promptly, yet Helen picks up a slight feeling of uncertainty. It is so tempting to trust Bill's reassuring words. But Helen knows that when words and feelings do not match, it is wiser to believe the feelings. So Helen works nonstop until she has a contingency plan. In a day, when it becomes obvious that Bill cannot deliver on his promise. Helen's contingency plan saves the show.

If someone tells you, "I love you," and her/his feelings are broadcasting, "I hate your guts", you better believe the feelings, because they cannot disguise as words do.

No emotion means no action.

> *Your Emotions cause action in decisions. Other players, including your Mind and Imagination, can move you into actions only if they trigger your Emotions.*

In decisions, when you are considering an option, your feelings vote on it either encouraging you to move on this option -- to hire a person, to enter a partnership -- or warning you to stay away from it. Since your Emotions fuel action, you must take into account their vote. If they are opposed to an option, you will not have enough energy to act on this option. To implement a decision you need full support of your Emotions.

What can you do if your Emotions are opposed to your decision? You can, for instance, invite your Emotions for a dialog in your Imagination. Ask what exactly they are opposed to or what makes them opposed. Appreciate the information your Emotions offer and check it out. You may discover that the decision you chose is not quite right for you or that the timing for this decision is off. You may discover another chink in your armor. (Later in this chapter you will learn techniques for eliciting more decision-making information from specific emotions). After you strengthened your weak points, your Emotions may happily align with your decision.

> *Never undervalue the information emotions deliver; never undervalue the power of emotions to cause action.*

If you react to any issue with strong emotions, it's a signal to change your approach to this issue without delay.

WHERE YOU NEED TO CHANGE YOUR APPROACH

> ➢ In which area (e.g., health, finances, career, education, relationships) do strong emotions come up for you?
> ➢ What would you want to achieve in this area?
> ➢ Come up with three new approaches that may move you where you want to be in this area.

Strong Emotions also announce, "A lot of energy is available to you right now!" Use that energy to explore available options or create new options for yourself. The presence of strong Emotions also warns you, "Caution! Calm down before making a decision." Later in this chapter you will find techniques for restoring emotional balance quickly. But first, examine your personal emotional profile.

Your Emotional Profile

While everyone might experience any emotion, each of us exhibits specific emotional habits. We will call them Predominant Emotional Patterns or PEPs. PEPs are the emotions with which you habitually react to challenges. Some people are in a habit of reacting with anger, others with guilt, still others with irritation. Happy children respond with joyous anticipation.

> ➢ To discover your PEPs, on the list of emotions at the end of this chapter (Chart 5.2) find the emotions which

show up for you most often or those which disturb you most in yourself or others. Those are your PEPs.

> *The harnessing of different emotions calls for different strategies. That is why you want to recognize quickly specific emotions in yourself and others.*

On Chart 5.3 at the end of the chapter, emotions are arranged into "families." In your journal, answer the following:

➤ Do all your PEPs come from one "family?"
➤ What's your main PEP (the one that bothers you most)?
➤ Which emotions belong to the "family" of your main PEP ?
➤ What insights does this information bring forth for you?
➤ How do you usually express your PEPs?
➤ How does your PEP change your speech, voice, face?
➤ How does your Body, its posture and movements change?
➤ In your Body, where and how do you feel emotional upsets and "highs"?
➤ What are the PEPs of two people closest to you?

When you know your "emotional portrait," you can more easily benefit from your moments of power. Later in this chapter you will find techniques for using specific emotions to support sound decisions

When Emotions Take You for a Ride

> *Whenever you lose sight of your goal – <u>inevitably</u> -- your Emotions will take you for a ride.*

Chapter 5

It happens with the best; it happens with the rest. Here is Denis, a successful and shrewd businessman who never once lost his focus in pursuing his business goals. But now he is bogged down in a messy divorce. His marriage was as oppressive as heavy chains and he wanted to end it as quickly as possible. Instead, he was stuck in endless divorce proceedings. Why? Denis has lost sight of his goal which was to free himself so he could start a new life. Instead, he and his wife, like many divorcing couples caught in mutual blame, resentment and vindictive emotions, found themselves entangled in divorce procedures that tied them to each other for years. Carried away with emotions, they forgot that their goal was not to square accounts with each other.

In the "trial of the century" we saw how O.J. Simpson's defense skillfully triggered powerful emotions that kept fogging the goal of the trial. Losing track of the goal in the emotional fog happens over, and over, and over in all areas of life -- relationships, politics, business, you name it. Look around: people start discussing ways to get to a goal, emotions come up (often around minor issues or details) and goals move out of focus until forgotten.

To avoid the mistake of losing sight of your goal, keep asking yourself,

> ➢ What is my goal here? What do I really want to achieve through my choices and actions?
> ➢ Which Emotions come up for me around my current decision?
> ➢ How can I use those Emotions to support my goal?

When Denis got these questions, his Mind immediately refocused on his goal of getting out of the marriage. The fog of vindictive feelings lifted, and Denis was stunned to realize how much time, energy and money he has spent to hold on to his chains. What an irony! Denis laughed at himself. Immediately he knew that all the disputed property was not worth another minute of carrying his chains.

Misidentification

It is the most common way to let emotions take us for a ride. We identify with something less than we are and we get emotionally attached to what we identified with. Some people identify with their feelings. When their feelings are not appreciated, they themselves feel unappreciated. Others identify with their ideas. If those ideas are rejected, they themselves feel rejected. Still others get attached to positions they hold and if they lose those positions, they feel devastated. There are people who identify with places and/or roles in life. I remember how, in my early years in the US, I read an article that portrayed Russian people as ridiculously ignorant and unlovable. Although the author herself was blatantly ignorant of Russia and biased, I got deeply upset. Obviously, I was still identifying with Russia. All those misidentifications are signs of emotional immaturity.

> *When we mature emotionally, we take full responsibility for our emotions and we keep our inner environment positive.*

We realize that our positions, ideas, and roles are just few among millions of our experiences, and we are far greater than all of our outer expressions and achievements.

> *Emotional maturity means being emotionally self-supportive.*

Chapter 5

To avoid misidentifying with the transient and insignificant, you may want to identify with any of the Coach's faces, for instance, with peace, freedom or joy (see chart 3 at the end of chapter 2.) Or, you can identify with a great spiritual master or even with the Supreme Being. To maintain the right identification requires awareness and constant vigilance. When we lose them, we fall into emotional traps.

Emotional traps

Trap #1: Blaming others.
Blaming others is a blatant sign of emotional immaturity. When life does not unfold to his liking, the emotionally immature decision-maker blames others, not realizing that the blaming renders him powerless. "They did it. I can do nothing about it." At his own volition, he turns himself into a victim and he receives what goes along with playing victim -- self-pity, resentment, anger, frustration, even rage.

Emotional maturity is not determined by age or education, as the case of Jose in the following example illustrates. For ten years Jose was saving money for the first new car in his life. But the car proved to be a lemon. All Jose's friends told him, "You'll have to live with it." But Jose managed to find a lawyer who agreed to challenge the manufacturer. After a year-long legal struggle with an auto giant, to the great surprise of many, Jose's lawyer won. The automaker took the car back and fully refunded the money. Semi-illiterate and short of money Jose, instead of blaming others and getting embittered, took an emotionally mature non-victim stand in life.

Trap #2: Predicating Your Decisions on Other People's Change.
When the emotionally immature decision-maker stumbles over an obstacle, he demands that others change so he can

proceed. As we mature emotionally, we see the funny side of this trap. The one who attempts to change others is in fact saying, "I want *you* to change, so I myself don't have to change." People change according to their own pace. Attempts to control that pace generate endless frustration. So, when the emotionally mature decision-maker encounters obstacles, he fluidly changes his plan, like a river flowing around boulders and islets.

Trap #3: Letting Others Decide for You.

It is, in a sense, the other side of the "blaming others" coin. If you let others decide for you or put them on a pedestal, you render yourself powerless by telling yourself "I don't have their knowledge and power. Anyway, they know better." The emotionally immature decision-maker does it, especially, around authority figures and/or experts. In a childish hope that a doctor, lawyer or spiritual master will take care of his needs, as did mommy and daddy when he was a baby, he follows their advice and opinions disregarding his own decision clues and his own knowing.

Don't you, an emotionally mature decision-maker, turn to experts for advice? Of course, you do. You listen to them with an open mind, paying close attention to how your decision team responds. You ask questions; you probe further when your signals do not align with their recommendations. You notice what they say, how they say it. what they avoid discussing and whether they hedge and fudge. As they talk, you watch how your Body responds, what images pop up, what feelings come up. Always remember: you are the one who lives in your Body. It is your life, and you are the one who will live the consequences of your decisions.

Chapter 5

> *You are the top authority over your life. Make sure your decisions are aligned with your inner compass team.*

Trap #4 Holding on to negative feelings.

Sometimes people are attached to their emotional drama and negative emotions. People get angry when someone attempts to free them from their negativity, like horror movie lovers get angry if someone turns on the lights before the movie ends. Yet, negative emotions poison you. By keeping them, you make your Body sick (2).

> *Your negative feelings chain you to the very people and situations that disturb you.*

The chains of emotional control defy time and space. Indeed, you may hold a grudge over something that happened decades ago and hate someone who is thousand miles away. Each time you recall a hurt or another emotional disturbance, you reinforce the chains of emotional control. These chains seem indestructible. Fortunately, they are not. You may discover for yourself what good psychiatrists, priests, writers and other students of human consciousness knew all along:

> *Forgiveness dissolves the prison of emotional control.*

Do not let religious connotations of the word "forgiveness" dissuade you. Test forgiveness out. Say:
> ➤ I forgive myself for... (actions or inaction you judged)
> ➤ I forgive myself for judging my action/inaction as bad or wrong
> ➤ I forgive so and so... (those who hurt or upset you)

94

➢ I forgive myself for judging them/ what they did as bad /wrong

➢ You may discover that what you judged as "bad" led to good things. In a classic story, a peasant's horse ran away, and the man judged it as bad. The horse returned and brought with him two mares. Excited, the peasant judged that as good. But the next day his son was thrown off the horse's back and broke his leg. The peasant cried and called that bad. But soon all the young men in the area were drafted to fight a war. The peasant's son was spared, because his leg was broken. Etc.

What exactly do you need to forgive? You need to forgive your judgments. We see just a tiny part of the whole picture -- it is so ignorant to judge. Yet, we keep on judging as part of human condition.

We may not understand how forgiveness works. Often, it seems impossible to forgive. Yet, the experience shows that if we keep a clear intention to forgive, we release negative emotions and dissolve the chains of emotional control. Many of our judgments dropped into the unconscious. So, you may want to include this line: "I forgive myself for judgments of which I'm not conscious." If you truly want inner freedom, keep forgiving: There is an immediate advantage in forgiving.

> *The one who manages to forgive first is rewarded with freedom. S/he has dissolved the chains of the past. S/he gained the freedom to move forward.*

Free yourself from the emotional habits that run you.

When we mature emotionally, we may free ourselves from a predominant emotional pattern (PEP) that used to run our life, whether it is a habit of getting angry, being possessive, feeling rejected or another one.

For instance, if feeling rejected is my PEP, then I perceive whatever is happening in my life through the prism of rejection. I may feel rejected whether rejection is there or not. I wasn't admitted to a certain university department - "They rejected me." I had to emigrate -- my native country rejected me. A charity refused my donation, saying they were overstocked and didn't accept donations anymore --I felt rejected. How do we free ourselves from this tyranny of a PEP?

A big step toward freedom is realizing how well that PEP served us. Rejected by the biology department, I had to major in exact sciences, which brought me a successful career. Emigration -- jumping from the prestigious status of an associate professor in the capital of the Soviet Empire to that of a poor immigrant without language, money, connections and friends in the West -- afforded me a rich experience of growth. Did I feel rejected! Rejected because of my accent, because of not knowing local customs, because of viewing and doing things differently, etc., etc. Such a huge dose of rejection challenged me to find the strongest antidote to my PEP, so I'd become free to be me. The pain of rejection shook the extraneous out of me in a hurry. I could not soothe that pain of rejection with anything less than reaching into my joyful, loving, and absolutely free spirit. Then the deepest reverence for the indomitable spirit that lives in our hearts emerged. *Identifying with this spirit in myself and others became my antidote.*

Once I saw how the pattern of rejection served me, I felt gratitude for having had it. The gratitude marked completion. The pattern of rejection lost its grip over me. (Some people may want the guidance of a qualified psychologist to get free from an emotional pattern.)

A radical way to complete a PEP is to start loving yourself unconditionally. But how can we when we are so used to judging ourselves unconditionally?

> *The ability to love yourself comes with forgiveness.*

As we forgive, we get in touch with our humanness as well as with the part of us we call the "Coach" which remains at peace, joyful, free and entirely lovable no matter what mistakes or how many we make.

Are Pessimists and Optimists Equally Good at Decisions?

While both pessimists and optimists are aware of negativity, optimists choose to focus on the bright side. How much do those attitudes really matter? In decisions, your attitude can be a matter of life and death, as a recent event dramatically illustrated.

A private airplane crashed. Three survivors had to wander in a forest for days until they were rescued. Jack lost his mind; Peter was found dead. Tom came out of the accident stronger than ever. What kind of people were those three men? Coworkers remembered Jack as a pessimist, convinced that the world was out to get him. They remembered Peter as a man who had believed only in himself. The rescue crew found in Peter's pocket his diary from which they learned how lonely he had felt in the forest -- one man against huge indifferent nature. When he injured his leg, he figured that no one could arrive soon enough to help him and he stopped his attempts to survive. Tom's outlook was different. He had always lived as if there were a miracle waiting for him around the corner. During his wanderings in the forest, a poisonous snake bit him. He told us what happened. "I was so hungry, so anxious to eat the red berries I spotted that I failed to notice a rattlesnake. When he bit my finger, I dropped the berries, sucked the wound and spit. I had to cut off quickly my own flesh so my blood would flush out snake's poison before it spread through my body. Blood was coming strong. So I ripped my shirt and with a piece of it bandaged my wound. After all that, I felt so tired that I had to rest. As I was resting half-asleep under a big tree, a picture of those red berries from an old field handbook popped into my mind. The berries were highly poisonous! So the snake had saved my life. I felt deeply thankful, and somehow protected. I was ready to continue my journey."

Jack, Peter and Tom exemplified three basic attitudes:
"The world is against me,"
"The world is neutral, it doesn't care one way or the other,"
"The universe always plots to do me something ... good."
The last one is the attitude of success. By focusing on the positive, it deepens your joy, freedom and peace and *opens you to the cornucopia of the universe.*

There is a connection between the attitude of success and the ability to forgive.

> *The attitude of success with its positive focus, acceptance, and cooperation does not develop in an unforgiving person.*

Inner Peace

How often have you been a hostage to emotions at home, at work, in public places? There is a quality that assures that you are less likely to be swayed by emotions and, if you are, that you restore your equilibrium fast. This masterful trait, called "emotional stability," enables you to decide out of peace and awareness no matter what turmoil storms outside or inside. Emotional stability frees you from being hostage to emotions

> *Emotional stability is not predicated on circumstances.*

Indeed, one may experience emotional upheaval within a serene rural setting and maintain calm while rescuing people from burning houses.

INCREASE YOUR EMOTIONAL STABILITY

In your journal, jot answers to these questions:

➢ Who is your ideal of emotional stability? It can be a person, combination of people, movie character, literary personage, or fantasy

➢ What do you think your ideal is feeling in emotional situations?

➢ What enhances your emotional stability? List only things under your control (e.g., making others behave the way you like isn't under your control, while getting enough rest is)

➢ Around what people and situations do you become emotional?

➢ Think of a situation when you lost your cool. Had you maintained it, how would you have handled that situation?

➢ Create an image of yourself as emotionally stable as you would like to be

➢ Apply chapter 4 techniques of upgrading self-image to become as emotionally stable as you wish

Chapter 5

When strong winds blow, tree branches bend. But if the roots are deep and the trunk flexible, the tree remains intact. So can you maintain your inner peace intact while branches of your consciousness are caught in turmoil. The state of peace exists always. As during the mightiest storms, beneath huge ocean waves the water remains still, so it is with you. Even during the most shattering emotional storms, part of you, which is the "Coach," remains still. Beneath your tumultuous emotions lives peace. How do you find it? By turning your attention to peace. It sounds simple. But to evoke peace by simply turning your attention to it, *you need to have developed intimacy with peace.* You can develop it by becoming as absorbed in peace, stillness and quiet as the military are absorbed in wars.

In sports, in order to win you keep your eyes on the ball.

> *To win in decision-making, keep your focus on inner peace. Once you shift your attention to the storms, your emotional stability is gone, and you become hostage to emotional blackmail, hype, and hysteria.*

In sports, the habit of keeping your eyes on the ball comes from years of practicing. Similarly, the habit of keeping inner peace comes when you practice, practice and practice making decisions, under circumstances that challenge your emotional stability and inner peace.

Out of curiosity, how much time have you put so far into developing your inner peace and emotional stability? True, emotional stability wasn't part of the school curriculum. Nor was it emphasized as a prerequisite to being a good decision-maker, not even for world leaders. So, throughout history, individuals, groups, and entire countries keep finding themselves hostages to someone's paranoiac fear and morbid hatred. In the era of nuclear weapons, the misuse of emotions may turn our entire civilization into a hostage. So, it has become crucial for our survival to master emotional stability.

> *Develop the habit of being at peace. Then in moments of alarm, your attention automatically turns to peace, not to commotion. When you need peace most, you receive peace. It makes sense, doesn't it?*

EXPLORE YOUR INNER PEACE

Answer in your journal:
➤ What helps you keep your inner peace?
➤ What takes your attention off your inner peace?
➤ What helps you restore your inner peace? What are your quickest ways to do that (focus on breathing, think of a child or pet you love, other)
➤ While making a decision, do you take into account whether it will increase your peace and emotional stability? (never, rarely, often, usually, always)

During crises, emotionally stable people become peacemakers. In 1985, a psychotic woman took a rifle and went on a shooting spree in a suburban Philadelphia shopping mall. She kept killing children and adults, until a quiet young man took the rifle from her. He wanted to become a police officer. In preparation for that, he had been training himself to remain calm amidst danger. In times of severe storms the habit of being peaceful maintains the tree of life intact.

Your protection in emotional situations.

> *When strong negative emotions surge, often the best protection is to leave.*

If that is impossible:

Move into observation.

Suspend actions, judgments, evaluations. Instead of rushing, pushing, doing, deciding, relax placing no demands on self or others. Nothing is required -- just be a spectator, simply watching, having fun, viewing everyone as an actor on a stage. You don't even need to form any opinions.

Soon you may find yourself feeling grateful for the dedication with which the actors create this show for you so you can learn to handle certain patterns of behavior. Indeed, in heated situations on the job or in the family observation *helps you have a good time and find wise options.* Once you've begun observing, you've raised your perspective. You are now looking from above at the boiling, churning, swirling stream called "emotions." True observation evokes peace. Once you feel peace, people around you may calm down without you doing anything outwardly. Out of inner stillness you may see how to resolve the situation without hurting anyone.

> *Quiet observation has the power to set you free.*

Humor.

Humor discharges emotional thunder clouds. To evoke humor when you need it most, say, when you feel embarrassed or intimidated, you can, for instance, exaggerate your own reactions, or talk about yourself in the third person. On developing humor see, for instance, (3).

The White Light Technique.

Let your Imagination fill you with pure white light. Let it surround you with a strong protective shield of white light. Then place this light with everyone else in the situation, asking that only that which is for your highest good come forward.

To use this strategy, you do not need to believe anything. Just have a willingness to apply your Imagination and experiment with a resource you may not have used yet. You may find a favorable change in yourself and the situation. The ideal is to keep yourself in a protective capsule of pure white light always.

Healthy Ways to Release Emotional Build-Up.

When you feel overwhelmed by emotions, dumping them on others only aggravates the situation and repressing emotions creates psychological problems. Here are some healthy ways to bring emotional energy to a level you can handle:

> Do hard physical work. In advance, list energy-consuming physical chores you need to do. When anger shows up, use its energy to do the chores
> Do the gardening so that you touch dirt with your hands and bare feet. Or, walk barefoot on the grass, dirt, or beach for 10-15 minutes
> Run around the block or engage in other energetic sports
> Take a cold shower

How to Benefit from
Your Anger, Frustration and Resentment

Anger .

Anger often carries so much energy, that first, you may need to release its excess as described above. Then, ask yourself:

> ➤ What angers me most in this situation?
> ➤ What do I really want here?
> ➤ Do I demand that others change?
> ➤ How can *I* change *my* approach/perspective/attitude to get what I want, acting out of respect for myself and others?
> ➤ Then go about getting what you really want.

Frustration .
Frustration signals a futile wish to change the past and/or useless judgments of how things are. To get what you want use the above strategy for anger, replacing the word "anger" with the word "frustration."

Irritation.
Use the strategy for anger, replacing the word "anger" with the word "irritation."

Jealousy, possessiveness.
If you really love him/her, you'd be grateful to whoever brings him/her joy. Ask yourself:

> ➤ What do I want from him/her?
> ➤ How can I myself get it?
> ➤ What attracts him/her in that other person?
> ➤ How did that person achieve what I'd like to achieve?
> ➤ Do I want to develop more of those traits?
> ➤ If yes, how can I do that?
> ➤ Why am I afraid to lose him/her?
> ➤ Where do I depend on him/her?
> ➤ What do I need to do to become more independent?

Resentment.
An emotion on its own, resentment often accompanies other negative emotions. We contract resentment when we

move our attention away from peace into the terrain of separation, where ego rules. Ego is a joint venture of the emotions and the mind. When anything does not go exactly how our ego wanted, our ego takes it personally, blames it on someone -- "You hurt me, you are wrong!" -- and gives birth to resentment. We feed resentment by recreating in the imagination the situation where resentment was born. We repeat with determination deserving a better use such resentful phrases as:

"I'll show you how wrong you are!

You are not good enough for me. "

As we imagine that situation over and over, the stomach, back and neck tighten and we get headaches. When we repress resentment into the unconscious, we create insomnia and even compulsive and obsessive behavior. Few people realize how insidiously resentment poisons us and how far its repercussions reach. In decisions, it may cripple us to such a degree that we feel unable to take any actions. Resentment also badly distorts our judgment, even of those people and situations that we do not resent (4).

Once we have stepped into resentment, anything can trigger more resentment: "they" are too smart, too dumb, too thin, too fat, too perfect, too imperfect, too handsome, too ugly. We may even resent people who heal and teach us! How, then, do we ever get out of resentment? We do it through forgiveness.

> *Resentment is as much a part of human condition as the body odor. We clean out resentments with the waters of forgiveness.*

You may want to forgive wholeheartedly:

> ➤ I forgive myself for feeling resentful
> ➤ I forgive myself for judging my feelings of resentment
> ➤ Draw a deep breath

When doing forgiveness -- as opposed to just reading about it -- we discover its magic. We also discover that we forget to use it. That is why this chapter reminds you of forgiveness a few times.

Can resentment help you make sound decisions? Absolutely! Used correctly, resentments reveal valuable information. Give yourself a gift of time for the following exercise. It may bring you not only insights but also energy and healing.

INTELLIGENT USE OF RESENTMENTS

> ➤ Think of a person you resent
> ➤ For what do you resent her/him?
> ➤ Prescribe what and how s/he should have done better
> ➤ Where are you doing/ did/ wanted to do but didn't dare something similar to what you resent her/him for? If nothing pops up, check the areas of your life that concern or trouble you
> ➤ List your reasons for not having handled the area (s) of your life
> ➤ Apply your prescription for her/him to yourself
> ➤ What part of you does this person represent?
> ➤ Forgive yourself for resentment and judgment. After all, you only manifested a human condition
> ➤ Forgive that person
> ➤ Appreciate yourself for learning
> ➤ Where in your Body do you feel the appreciation?

Your Emotional Hygiene

> *Having the emotional layer of consciousness guarantees that we pick up negative emotions. If not eliminated, they poison us, no matter how healthy our diet or how well we exercise.*

To clean out your negative feelings take an emotional shower. When? Before falling asleep in the evening or any time. Emotional hygiene clears negative feelings and brings you self-loving and peace. Any time is good for doing that.

DURING AN EMOTIONAL SHOWER:

> ➤ make a list of people whom you resent, of whom you are jealous, with whom you are angry, frustrated, or experience any other negative emotions
> ➤ use the above techniques to clear those emotions
> ➤ forgive yourself
> ➤ forgive whoever bothers you
> ➤ imagine rinsing yourself and the people involved with pure peaceful white light
> ➤ let your Imagination feel the greatest Love holding and cuddling you as a much loved child
> ➤ appreciate yourself for anything good you did/felt today and make sure that your Body receives the appreciation

For more techniques on clearing various negative emotions out of your system see references (2) and (5-7).

If the debris of the food we eat are not eliminated, accidents happen. Same with your Emotions. If your negative feelings are not washed away, at the moment you need all your decision power, you may get sick physically, fall into depression, or explode with rage. Daily emotional showers dissolve the poisons of negative feelings, strengthening your immune system and overall health. Emotional showers also help make sound decisions, since the "cleaner" your Emotions, the better they communicate decision clues.

> *Your emotional hygiene is at least as important as your Body's hygiene.*

The mercurial character of your Emotions lets them bring you both decision clues and energy instantly. Their character also lets them take over your decision team instantly. The moment you loose your vigilance, emotions, can shake you, usually, at the most inconvenient times. No one is exempt. So, use the following two sections to refresh your vigilance.

Exclusive Interview with GMM – Great Masters of Misery.
(inspired by the manual on misery (8)

AUTHOR: What causes misery?
GMM #1: Negative thoughts do.
GMM #2: So do irrational beliefs.
AUTHOR: Would you give an example of such a belief?
GMM #2: Gladly. Here is a good one: "If I am a really good person, everyone will love me, appreciate me and approve of me."
AUTHOR: How else do we create misery?
GMM #3: One superb way: is to set up expectations of how people and things should be and take any deviation from your expectations as an affront.
GMM #1: My favorite way: when someone is upset, get upset also. Two upset people can surely create more misery than one.

GMM #2: Yes, I like nice people who feel guilty for being happy when I am miserable. They really help spread misery.

AUTHOR: What keeps us stuck in misery?

GMM #3 Fault-finding never fails to enrich misery for self and others.

GMM #2: Also, when blaming others, never end with blaming only your loved ones. The more people you blame the better.

AUTHOR: Your dedication to misery is truly remarkable. Thank you.

Checklist to avoid emotional traps

> ➤ Which of the misery-causing instructions do you still follow:
> ➤ a/ keep negative thoughts and irrational beliefs,
> ➤ b/ expect others to behave according to your specifications,
> ➤ c/ get upset because someone else is upset,
> ➤ d/ find faults,
> ➤ e/ other...?
> ➤ Do you blame someone in regard to your current decision?
> ➤ Are you counting on someone to change so you can reach your goal?
> ➤ What or whom have _you_ granted the power to be an obstacle to reaching your current goal?
> ➤ Are you letting someone decide for you?
> ➤ Are you choosing someone's recommendations over your own knowing?
> ➤ When interacting with people, are you aware of your Emotions?

➤ When interacting with others, are you aware of other people's feelings?

➤ Do you take into account how you <u>feel</u> about your decision?

➤ Are you holding on to negative feelings? Forgive and be free!

➤ When strong Emotions are present, what are they telling you? Do you take a moment to balance yourself before making a decision?

➤ If emotions keep flaring up, do you change your approach?

➤ When stumbling over an obstacle, do you remember that the world always plots to do you something... good?

➤ Are you keeping your eyes on your goal?

➤ Are you identifying with your Coach?

Re read this chapter and add to this checklist whatever especially helps *you* benefit from your emotions.

Summary

Emotions are to decisions what water is to Earth. Never underestimate the power and usefulness of the Emotions. Emotions -- positive and negative as well -- supply energy and vital decision-making clues. Use them to lift yourself and move to your goal.

FACES of the EMOTIONS

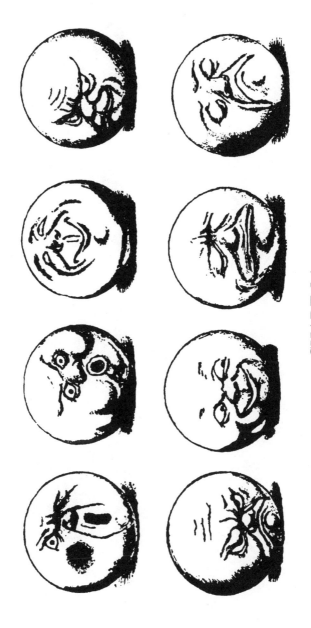

CHART 5.1

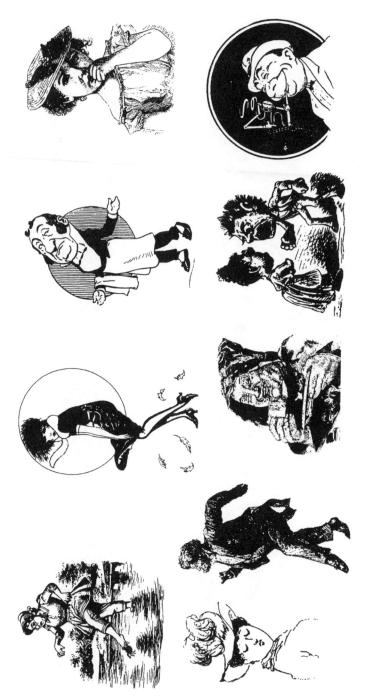

CHART 5.2

"FAMILIES" of the EMOTIONS

FEAR, HORROR, TERROR

◆

ARROGANCE, CONTEMPT, DISDAIN, SNEERING, DISGUST, SYMPATHY,
SELF-PITY, EMBARRASSMENT, SHAME, GUILT

◆

IMPATIENCE, ANNOYANCE, IRRITATION, INDIGNATION, RESENTMENT,
BITTERNESS, EXASPERATION, ANGER, VINDICTIVENESS, WRATH,
RAGE, FURY

◆

JEALOUSY, ENVY, GREED, POSSESSIVENESS

◆

HOSTILITY, ANIMOSITY, SPITE, HATRED, MALEVOLENCE, MALICE

◆

LACK, NEEDINESS, ABANDONMENT, LONELINESS, UNWORTHINESS,
REJECTION, GRIEF, SEPARATION

◆

WORRY, DISTRUST, DEFENSIVENESS, INSECURITY, ANXIETY

◆

DISAPPOINTMENT, FRUSTRATION, DISCOURAGEMENT,
DEPRESSION, DESPAIR, LETHARGY

◆

EXCITEMENT, EUPHORIA, ELATION, ENTHUSIASM,
HAPPINESS, ECSTASY, JOY, BLISS

CHART 5.3

6

Genius at Your Service

This chapter tells you how to avoid traps of the mind and enjoy its genius in decisions.

The Fourth Player -- Your Mind

One of the medieval legends describes the Golem as a robot-like servant created by a famous rabbi in Prague to do chores around the synagogue. Each morning the rabbi would put a piece of paper with instructions into the Golem's mouth, the Golem would do a great job, and at the end of the day, the rabbi would remove the instructions. But one day the Golem was left on its own and it took off running through the streets of Prague, creating havoc.

That Golem is a nice metaphor for the mind which is, indeed, a great servant but a poor master. Those who use the mind in decisions as master, get trapped by it.

> *When you look to the Coach as your master and your Mind as a servant, you can have at your service a genius .*

The slowest of the inner compass dimensions, the human mind nevertheless enjoys the highest prestige in Western culture. The mind's logic is portrayed as *the* decision-maker and treated as omniscient. It is not. <u>Unless specifically trained,</u> the mind overvalues its own tools -- words, numbers and logic. At the same time the mind greatly undervalues the imagination, ignores the body wisdom and treats emotions as abstract concepts. Have you seen the minds reasoning with the emotions when all the emotions want is to feel loved and appreciated? Your logical Mind is unaware of your own Unconscious and views with suspicion your intuition -- your Coach's instantaneous knowing. So much for the mind's omniscience.

Where then did the belief in the omniscience of the mind originate? Beliefs are under the dominion of the mind. So, it is the mind itself that promotes the belief in its own omniscience. It is "a paid political announcement!" Worse yet, the mind has bought into its own propaganda, into its grand illusion -- "I-KNOW-IT-ALL!" The grand illusion begets numerous mental traps. Over and over, you fall into them until you learn to recognize the traps and take advantage of them. In the next section use the genius of your Mind to take advantage of two traps -- judgments and assumptions.

Genius Reveals Your Hidden Roadblocks

The major mental trap is judgment differs from evaluation.

> *Evaluation is neutral, whereas judgment implies that the world should be different*

Judgment labels everything and everyone as "good" or "bad," "right" or "wrong," and in its smug ignorance, lectures everyone, including God, on how to behave. Judgment weakens your decision-making in many ways. It tightens your Body, reduces your awareness, shuts down your opportunities.

> *While judging, that is prescribing to others how to live their life, you miss out on your own life.*

Judgments also slow down your decision-making, because you need time to overcome the judgments you've made. Losing time in decision-making can be deadly. Nancy, a stockbroker, learned that from a tragic experience. Her daughter Savannah, fun-loving and very good-looking, was always surrounded with suave admirers. Among them, 5'4" Peter, dressed as though his clothes belonged to someone else bigger and richer, seemed out of place. Nancy judged Peter as unimportant. When he told her that Savannah had become involved with a dangerous drug dealer, Nancy dismissed his message as nonsense. Soon, very soon in fact, she woke up to Peter's message. Too late. Savannah disappeared and was never found.

Can your Mind stop judging entirely? That is unlikely. But you can use your judgments to discover hidden roadblocks.

> *Your judgments stem from your own imbalances that are your roadblocks, currently obstructing your movement.*

These roadblocks are often hidden from your awareness, although they may be obvious to others. That was the case when former First Lady Betty Ford entered group therapy to treat her alcohol addiction. She recalls how much she judged those who would not admit openly that they were alcoholics. Finally, it dawned on her that she herself was doing exactly what she judged -- she kept denying her own alcoholism. That denial was her major roadblock. Once she admitted her alcoholism, her recovery began in earnest (2). *Your judgments reveal chinks in your armor.*

My client Rhoda, a single parent and a computer store owner argued that she judged people for being irresponsible, but nobody would call her irresponsible. A closer look revealed, however, that Rhoda, at the expense of the much needed rest, kept handling tasks left unfinished by her sons at home and her employees at her store. She acted irresponsibly toward herself. Now Rhoda takes rest when she needs it -- a major achievement for a workaholic.

What indicates that *you have cleared an imbalance*? You have *if whatever used to trigger your judgments now registers in you without any emotional charge or "good"/"bad" labels.* For Betty Ford, after her rehabilitation, the word "alcoholic" lost its emotional charge of shame and disgrace.

TAKE ADVANTAGE OF YOUR JUDGMENTS

> ➤ What do you especially judge in people?
> ➤ Do you judge yourself for the same thing?
> ➤ Have you ever wanted to do what you judge them for?
> ➤ Are you afraid you might do what they do?
> ➤ Do your judgments relate to an area of your life you have not taken care of?

Here is how it worked for Rhoda. After she allowed herself to rest, she felt ready for fun. Yet, when actually invited to a party, she reacted with, "I don't want to go and listen to that stupid blabber about relationships." Noticing a judgment in her reaction, she asked herself, "Do I have an imbalance in the area of relationships?" She admitted that she did. She was aching for a warm and intelligent companion. Had Rhoda had the area of relationships balanced, she might still not like wasting her time on "stupid blabber." But instead of judging it, she would probably just change the topic of conversation.

Uncover splendid options for your current decision

Uncover splendid options for your decision by challenging your assumptions. To assume means to take a statement for granted. For instance, after the defeat in World War II, Japan badly needed to import food. Yet, at that time, the Japanese goods known in the West were so shoddy that "made in Japan" was a warning not to buy. So, many Japanese assumed that:

⇒ Japan could not compete in international markets
⇒ the resources of the nation were negligible
⇒ Japan could not get the money to import food

When Japan hired Dr. Edward Deming, an American professor, he challenged all those assumptions. He identified as Japan's immediate resource the nation's industrious work force and the fine sense of quality, demonstrated in superbly made goods for the military. Since for the Japanese the quality of exports meant food on the table, they promptly adopted Deming's methods of quality control. Deming predicted that with them Japan would win international markets in five years. Japan did that in four. In 1951 Japan established the Deming prize -- a yearly award for quality control that became as prestigious and coveted as the Oscar in the USA.

UNCOVER OVERLOOKED OPTIONS FOR YOUR DECISION.

➢ Think of a decision you have been putting off
➢ Write down all your reasons for putting it off
➢ If those reasons magically vanish, how will you go about this decision?
➢ What limits you in this decision?
➢ Do those limits/ rules indeed exist?
➢ If yes, what are they based on?
➢ Who set them? Whom do they benefit?
➢ Fish out all your explicit and implicit assumptions
➢ Challenge each one of them

➤ What new opportunities have you found ?

When facing a decision, the mind often assumes that you have more and bigger obstacles than in fact you do and that you have fewer options and resources than you do. In other words, *the mind tends to exaggerate the difficulties you face.* Often, the mind adds difficulties by making up rules and limitations. For instance, it was an unspoken rule that in an art class of thirty only a few would learn drawing skills. Betty Edwards freed her mind from that rule. She has taught drawing on the right side of the brain, and in her classes all the students have learned to draw well (1).

Isn't it shocking to discover how many false assumptions we take for granted? And isn't it liberating to challenge your assumptions? Challenging assumptions does take time but so does stopping at red lights when driving.

How Much Information You Really Need

You really need to know only your next step. If you participate in your current step fully, the next one will reveal itself. All information for your next step is available right now through your inner compass.

> *More information does NOT equal more wisdom at all!*

GET INFORMATION FOR YOUR NEXT STEP:

➤ List your options
➤ One by one, imagine implementing your options and watch which options enhance your Body's well-being
➤ How do you *feel* about your options? What decision clues do these feelings offer?

120

➤ If you don't like your options, find other ones by challenging your assumptions about your next step

➤ Have your Imagination invite your role model, or a spiritual master, or the greatest in your field of endeavor and ask what next step they would take in your situation

➤ Move into action and watch how feedback from your team reveals your next step

That's what my friend Marty did when doctors recommended surgery to stop her internal bleeding. Marty was adamantly opposed to surgery. She turned to natural healing. Unfortunately, her bleeding continued and her hemoglobin level began to drop. Two months later she had to resort to surgery anyway. So, what did she gain through her action? She gained feedback from her Body that drastically changed her attitude toward surgery. Now she felt thankful that the surgical option was available to her. Sitting in the "should I/shouldn't I?" dilemma would not have produced such a benefit.

Do you realize how much information is available through your team? Chapters 7 and 8 reveal how to add input from your Unconscious and Coach.

Escape the traps of the mind that delay action

Unlike the emotions that impetuously push us into action, the logical mind tends to postpone action indefinitely, Fortunately, within your Mind, in addition to the logical Mind, lives your Intellect -- a liaison with your Coach -- that can move your logical Mind toward your goal. To help you detect traps of your logical Mind that delay action we will give some traps names and voices. We'll also give voice to your Intellect and Coach to advise you on how to avoid the traps.

Mentalizer: I love talking. I'd take talk over action any time. I like mental gymnastics, the juggling of words and numbers, opinions and data. I assign fancy terms to simple things and watch the terms cling together mushrooming into formidable professional jargons -- the legalese, the computerese, ad infinitum. Has someone added "ad nauseum?" Poor simpleton! Of course, mentalizing is not for simpletons. It's for the sophisticates who appreciate the gathering of information for the sake of information, who savor discussions about nothing in particular and good conversation for its own sake. To avoid action I demand many experts' opinions on any issue. The differences in their opinions naturally raise questions that trigger more questions, postponing action forever...

Intellect: Before asking a question, think whether an answer will help you move into action. If it can't, do not ask it.

Doubter: I doubt everything. So why bother doing anything?

Intellect: If in doubt, check it out. Checking out invigorates, and your doubt becomes a constructive one.

Understander: How can I move into action if I don't know in advance exactly what will be taking place and how? Before moving into action, I must understa-a-a-nd!

Coach: All you need to know is your first step. It will reveal what's next. Understanding comes after all your players have participated in the experience and learned from it. True understanding never precedes experience. Many questions can be answered only in action.

Fault-finder: Nobody is good enough. There isn't one single person who'd measure up! Who? Me? Nah... I am too ... old, young, fat, skinny, ugly, beautiful, underqualified, overqualified... fill in the blank. I'm inadequate. I can't do anything!

Perfectionist: I will do something only if I'm sure that I can do it perfectly. I am not going to play softball like a klutz. In fact I won't play until I can play perfectly.

Intellect: Success comes through action. Forget "I can't." Erase this phrase from your vocabulary. Replace it with "I AM DOING IT."

When to base your decisions on logic

Base on logic your decisions in the areas not affected by rapid change, such as decisions to diet, to keep inner peace or develop other great habits. Those decisions require follow-through choices. For instance, if you decided to diet, then at each meal you must make a follow-through choice to stick to that diet. Or, if you decided to feel happy, you must keep choosing happiness over misery. Yes, feeling happy is a decision, and its implementation depends on you -- not on your circumstances. Dr. H. Greenwald (3) recalls the unusual response of a patient who was just diagnosed with cancer and given six months to live. "Thank God," she exclaimed. "I don't need to worry about the future anymore. I can live the way I want to!" She did. She filled those last months of her life with happiness and did not even bother with check-ups. Half a year later her oncologist could not find any evidence of cancer, so he told her it was in remission. Once more she surprised him with her response, "Oh, no! Now I need to worry about the future again!" At that point, she realized that she did not need cancer to maintain her happiness. (If you decide to take charge of your happiness, you may find references 3-6 helpful.)

My client Christopher told me that for his 37th birthday, he gave himself two gifts -- a handsome sports car and the decision to be happy. His friends were impressed. The very next day someone bumped into his new car and bent a fender. Christopher got very upset. Suddenly, a thought popped up: "Wait a minute. I am on a date with my happiness." It was his mind's message. Christopher's logical mind reasoned that, upset or happy, he needed to fix his car anyway, so he might as well feel happy.

During follow-through choices, make sure to pay attention to your Body, Imagination and Emotions. They may get information not available to your Mind and send signals that warrant "changing your mind." Again, Christopher provides a good example. He had signed up for an evening course on interactive computers. As he was preparing to leave for the first class, he felt a sharp pain in his eye. His mind's logic pushed him to go. But when he imagined staying home, the pain vanished. Clearly, his body voted "no" on going to the class that evening. An hour later he received a phone call that resulted in getting the best job of his life. Fortunately, he honored his body's vote over his mind's logic. I myself learned that lesson from the university of hard knocks. Once I worked long hours away from home for a week. When the work was finished, my mind's logic demanded that I drove home right away. Without checking with my body, I hit the road and soon fell asleep behind the wheel. My car jumped off the road, waking up and scaring both me and my passenger. Luckily, we were on a deserted rural road and nobody got hurt. A cup of coffee at the nearest Howard Johnson's assured our uneventful return home. It was quite a lesson though. So, when making a follow-through choice, check with your players in this order:

⇒ find out how your Body votes

⇒ how you *feel* about the choice

⇒ only then get the opinion of your Mind

If you start with the Mind, it may sway the votes of your Body and Emotions.

When Your Logic Becomes a Trap

Let's start with this example. In the early 80s, investments were poured into thriving dairy farming in Northern Europe. But in 1986 nuclear disaster at Chernobyl (Ukraine) contaminated dairy products across Northern Europe, and the investments went down the drain. Logic could not have forewarned the investors. Logic is based on data. In this case the data needed could not have existed. Indeed, before the accident, who among European farmers or investors had ever heard of Chernobyl and why on earth would they have any concern about an obscure nuclear station, located far away in Ukraine? Moreover, in the experts' estimation, the probability that all the factors that caused the Chernobyl disaster would converge was one in a million!

Could anything have forewarned those investors? Definitely! Had they checked how the nonverbal players on their own personal decision teams reacted to the decision to make those investments, they might have gotten uneasy feelings, discomforts in the body and other warnings. Had they heeded those warnings, they would have stayed away from the ill-fated investment, although only in retrospect would they learn why. By comparison, you may remember from chapter 3 the example about Soros, a Wall Street investment wizard who created huge fortunes for himself and others. Soros listened to and took into account his body responses in choosing his investment strategies (7).

> *Logic of the mind traps us when our decisions concern areas of rapid unpredictable change.*

Like computers, your Mind has only the information that was put into it. That information can be extrapolated into the

future, but extrapolations forecast well only if things keep un-
folding the way they used to, which is now rarely the case. So,
it's worth repeating: the mind's logic can no longer predict the
outcomes of complex decisions. Why no longer? Because new
technologies have intertwined in countless ways previously unrelated areas of life in our "global village". As a result, new
factors which *the mind is not designed to foresee* enter into play
and determine the outcomes. The mind's premises are derived
from the past because that is the only information the mind has.
When the degree of newness is high, the mind's logic often
leads to wrong conclusions. The mind's logic becomes a trap
when *the mind applies premises, based on the past, to a future
that differs radically from that past.*

The example that illustrates the point comes from the Per-
sian Gulf War in 1990. Our media often portrayed Saddam
Hussein as irrational. Yet, he simply acted on these premises
well rooted in the past: a) once attacked, Israel would immediately retaliate, and b) the Arab members of the anti-Iraq coali-
tion would side with Iraq against Israel. Indeed, never once in
Israel's history had Israel failed to retaliate, and the Arab
countries have traditionally fallen prey to anti-Israel propaganda. Yet, new factors came into play, and when attacked by
Iraq in 1990, Israel exercised restraint and the anti-Iraq coali-
tion grew stronger.

How then do you handle decisions when your Mind's logic
does not apply? Rather than "making up your mind," get input
from other members of your team. Find out how your Body,
feelings and Imagination vote on this decision.

When facing radically new patterns, let the patterns themselves suggest ways of dealing with them. Switch to a receptive
mode. Tap your inner stillness and listen without bias or cen-
sorship. Chapters 8-10 explain how to use your inner compass

126

so that the future – not the past – guide your decisions. If however, you give the mind the role of the master, that is, of the chief decision-maker, it will impose old ways on the new flow. Then the mind is up against a task beyond its capacities. Where action is needed, the mind goes into information gathering, evaluation of pros and cons and "paralysis by analysis." As productivity drops, the mind judges everything, creating resentment, anger, blame and guilt. Then noble resolutions pave the way to hell.

Perhaps you've seen Rodin's famous sculpture "The Thinker." Do you know where Rodin placed it? At the very top of his composition "The Gates of Hell!"

Why the logical mind resists the new.

When substantial newness comes from the outside, the mind opposes it. Why does the mind support traditions and resist the new?

⇒ The mind is into control. Order and predictability, rules and structure help control, whereas newness brings uncertainty and chaos that turn meaningless the order and predictability the mind created.

⇒ The mind is slow compared to intuition (although compared to physical actions, thoughts are fast). All processes of the mind take time: it takes time to say words; it takes time to think; it takes time to go through logical steps. It takes time for the mind to accept the new.

⇒ The mind has absolutely no advance proof that the intuition is right. Let's consider examples. Some 500 years ago Leonardo Da Vinci asserted that man would fly in the sky like a bird. Can you imagine how absurd that appeared to the mind? Man could not even jump high enough! Or, some 80 years ago, who would have taken seriously the idea that from your living room you could watch events on the other side of the earth? The mind argues, "OK, those ideas happened to be true. Aviation and television did become part of our lives. But for each brilliant idea millions of crazy ones float around." That is true. Both genius and schizophrenic put together elements of reality in an unusual way, and the logical mind is not equipped to distinguish in advance between the brilliant and the crazy. That is why the mind has an uneasy relationship with the radical newness that intuition brings forward. Not by accident, history brims with brilliant discoveries and successes pioneered despite the logic of their time.

When a pioneer offers radically new premises, he has gotten them from a powerful eureka experience (see chapter 8) where the Coach brought forward a new knowing, lifting the entire team to new heights, to a bigger picture. During eureka the pioneer's mind got enlightened. But other people had no eureka. Based on their past knowledge, they deny the validity of the new. If the pioneer has the guts and stamina to follow his intuition, if despite the mocking shouts of the minds he introduces his discovery to the world, the validity of the new becomes evident. Then the mind, the proverbial Monday morning quarterback, explains with authority and impeccable logic why a certain premise was bound to prove right or a certain product was bound to succeed on the market.

The premises of the mind differ fundamentally from the premises suggested by intuition.

> *The mind draws its premises from the past, whereas*
>
> *intuition receives its premises from the future.*

Here is a classic example. When Dr. Land introduced his idea of the Polaroid camera, he encountered strong resistance from market analysts. They reasoned that since the Polaroid was too expensive to sell as a toy and its picture quality could not compete with regular cameras, the Polaroid had absolutely no chance on the market. Dr. Land went ahead anyway and became one of the biggest business successes of the 20th century. Where did the market analysts go wrong? They used this wrong premise: "The customer buys or rejects a camera based on its picture quality and price." That was true in the past. But in the past, instant photography did not exist. Intuitively, Dr. Land knew that the fun and instant gratification the Polaroid pictures offered would far outweigh their imperfections.

In predicting how a product will do on the market, market analysts encounter a major difficulty. The mind does not know which factors will be crucial when the product enters the market. So the mind cannot tell on which premises to base market analysis. But other than the mind members of the market analyst's personal decision team broadcast numerous clues.

Make sure the genius works for – not against – you.

Although the mind alone cannot make adequate decisions, it wields huge power in decision-making. Henry Ford summed it up this way: "Whether you say you can or you can't – either way you're right."

What you think determines how you feel about yourself and your life and what you can achieve.

Huge power of the mind stems from the universal law: *energy follows the thoughts you keep.* You can observe this law in action when you dwell on happy thoughts and your happiness increases. Your energy, following your thoughts, goes to your happiness. By the same token, if you keep thinking of your inadequacies, your energy, following your thoughts, deepens feelings of inadequacy. Indeed, we cannot afford the luxury of a negative thought (6). So be good to yourself. Keep thinking of what you want and your energy will go toward it. Then the law works for you as your persistent thoughts create a field of mental energy that triggers persistent imagery enlivening the mental field with colors and sights, sounds and smells. Your Emotions, triggered by the thoughts, nurture the field like water and sunshine nurture seeds in the soil. Persistent images make your Unconscious draw to you the resources you need. Once you move into action, your garden of results blossoms in a way that looks miraculous to those uninitiated into the law "energy follows thought."

Dr. Land cooperated with this law. He often contemplated how he could bring people more beauty. Once in New Mexico, he was taking pictures of his three-year-old daughter. She wanted to see them immediately. He said it wasn't possible. "Why?" she asked. At that instant, his child epitomized a common human desire to preserve the fun of the moment and enjoy the "preserve" right away. Her question translated for Dr. Land into a decision to invent a way to get instant pictures. He meditated on it for an hour with full concentration, entirely oblivious to the outer world. Within that hour, the idea of the Polaroid took shape. The idea came from an intuitive flash, but that flash did not appear just by luck. Dr. Land led himself to that breakthrough by thinking consistently of the means to bring people beauty.

> *The genius of the mind can create or destroy with equal power. It is up to you whether your Mind creates or destroys, supports or sabotages you.*

LOVING DISCIPLINE OF USING YOUR MIND POSITIVELY:

> ➢ at all times, savor the positive
> ➢ direct your thoughts to where you want to arrive
> ➢ focus on completing what you're doing
> ➢ direct your Imagination so it holds vibrant images of your success (8)

Some call the imagination "the theater of the mind." Make sure your "theater" stages only the shows that support you.

CHECK WHETHER YOUR MIND SUPPORTS YOU

> ➤ Is my focus positive?
> ➤ In my Imagination, am I experiencing myself the way I want to be?
> ➤ Am I enjoying thoughts and images of my success
> ➤ Am I directing my attention toward completing what I'm doing?

If the answer to the above is "yes, no room will be left for worries, depression or discouragement.

The universal law "energy follows thought" makes the mind the captain of decision-making team. The mind takes care of the team, like municipal authorities take care of a city. They maintain road repairs, garbage collection, public safety and other aspects of city life so that we can freely go about our business. Similarly, your Mind organizes your resources and stores the learning that builds your team's mastery. Your Mind records the knowledge you gain from your decision-making experience. Other players record information in their own way, but the mind's memory is the easiest to access.

It is said that success is 5% inspiration and 95% perspiration. The perspiration includes holding your thoughts on your goal long enough. Sir Isaac Newton, the genius who discovered, among other things, the first three laws of mechanics and the law of gravity, attributed his achievements to his ability to *hold thoughts on a given subject longer than most people do.* It is not easy. Intellectual laziness plagues the human race. That is why it is said that

five percent of all the people think;
fifteen percent think that they think;
the rest would rather die than think..

131

Chapter 6

How long can you hold your thoughts on one subject? Can you concentrate on it long enough for your lasered energies to crreate a breakthrough? That ability comes when you've done away with intellectual laziness and practice, practice, practice. Then your thinking becomes the cause of goodness you bring into your life.

The mind is a genius at organizing. Through classifying, planning, and clear-cut rules, the mind creates an order that conveys a comfortable sense of stability and security, a sense that the flow of events is predictable and reliable. With figures under its dominion, the mind thrives on quantifying, measuring and developing the how-tos of high productivity. Not by accident, the word "genius" is linked to the Latin "gignere," meaning "to produce."

Time and money are the mind's darlings. Easily measurable, the flow of time and the flow of money indicate to your Mind -- with precision -- how efficient your current approach to your goal is.

Habits are also darlings of the mind. The mind is designed to help us develop habits. Which habits would you want to have? A habit to complete what you start? A habit of treating yourself only in a respectful, compassionate and supportive way? Never underestimate the mighty force of habits to make your resources readily available to you or, if a habit is bad, to deplete your resources inexorably. Sometimes, a bad habit can be dropped through the sheer power of intellect, as J. Paul Getty, the legendary oil tycoon, did. He used to smoke heavily. Once, after motoring through France in a heavy rainstorm, he stopped for a night's rest in a small town hotel. In the middle of the night, he woke up craving a cigarette, but he had none. He wanted to smoke so badly that hc got out of bed, dressed fully, reached for his raincoat and suddenly realized how ridiculous his actions were. He was going to slosh a dozen blocks through freezing rain in the middle of the night to get a cigarette. His habit was running him! He rebelled mentally and right on the spot made a decision. With a sense of triumph he went back to sleep. He never smoked again (9). Can you rid yourself of a bad habit by "making up your mind?"

Great servant but a poor master

Have you observed how the mind gets so absorbed in its activities -- in its books, spreadsheets, laboratories and computers, or even in its very search for Truth -- that it misses Truth present here and now? Have you observed how in its fervor to serve an idea or a belief, the mind can rationalize, excuse and justify absolutely anything – cannibalism, war, torture? So make sure that your ideals, goals and strategies are aligned with your Coach. Keep turning to your Coach (see chapter 8). Your Coach can always restore the proper perspective. For instance, when the mind, in its pursuit of efficiency, grows fanatical, turns goals into gods and creates unbearable time pressures, the Coach may gently remind the Mind an old Irish saying,

> *When God created Time, He created enough of it.*

Questions Genius Asks.

How you ask your question determines where your energy goes.

TO HAVE YOUR ENERGY PROPEL YOU TO YOUR GOAL

ask:
> How can I use this obstacle to propel me to my goal?
> How can I use the strength of my opponent/competition to propel me to my goal?

‖➤ How can I use this challenge to deepen my freedom?

Once, I was to fly to Europe out of JFK Airport in New York. A door-to-door limousine scheduled to pick me up in Philadelphia. The limousine office kept assuring me that the limousine would be at my place any moment. Finally, it became obvious that the limousine had left for New York without me. The mind could have asked, How could you forget me? Who is at fault? etc. Fortunately, I asked instead, How can you get me to JFK on time? That question focused everyone's thoughts and energies on the only thing that mattered – catching my flight. (I did.)

> *Wrong questions focus on roadblocks; right questions focus your thoughts and energies on where you want to arrive.*

According to ancient Roman belief, genius is a tutelary deity, assigned to a person at birth. Genius is also associated with superior talent. When the genius of your Mind aligns with the Coach, you implement decisions that make your impossible dreams come true.

Summary

By its nature, the logical Mind resists the new. But when your Coach is the master, your Mind becomes a genius servant provided you have learned to avoid its traps and lovingly disciplined it to support you. Remember: what you think and tell yourself determines what you are able to do and how you feel about yourself and your life.

7

Mirrors That Help Make Instant Decisions and Heal Your Past

This chapter reveals how to cooperate with your Unconscious to gain freedom, energy and instant clues for your decisions.

Welcome to Your Unconscious, the Fifth Player

The fifth dimension of your inner compass – your Unconscious -- is your most influential and most mysterious player (chart 7.1 at the end of this chapter). It is your Unconscious that puts up special mirrors to help you make decisions and heal your past. We will use the term "Unconscious" to encompass both below-conscious levels -- your subconscious and, hidden even deeper in your psyche, the unconscious itself.

There is a difference between the two. The subconscious, or semi-conscious, stores information you have semi-forgotten. For instance, at the moment, I can't recall the name of my uncle. But I know that I know it. The memory of the name dropped below my conscious mind, into my subconscious. The name will surface when I stop pressing for it and relax.

Unlike your subconscious, your Unconscious stores what you are unconscious of, by definition. You may have no recall of some painful occurrences in your life. Their memories have sunk into your subconscious, then deeper down into the oblivion of your Unconscious. Does true oblivion exist, however? In its unique codes, your Unconscious records all your experiences. Under certain conditions, people recall, to their astonishment, the day they were born, who was present, what those people conversed about, what the weather was like. You may access other startling information you never knew you had. There is, indeed, much to astound you in the ocean-vast, deep and dynamic domain of your Unconscious.

What hooks you to your past.

Have you ever planned things to do and ended up doing something else, entirely different and hardly justifiable? Most of us have, and more than once. What causes that? Usually, incompletions recorded in your Unconscious do. Incompletions – the loose ends you left behind -- hook you to the past and lead your decisions astray.

An incompletion is anything you started and left "hanging" in any realm of consciousness. In the physical-material realm, incompletions are projects you worked on physically and then abandoned, like a boat you started building and left unfinished. In the mental and imaginative realms incompletions are thoughts and images upon which you dwelt and charged with feelings but neither implemented physically nor fully let go of. For instance, many people say, "I'll write a book." Some keep thinking of the ideas and experiences to include into the book. The images of the book get charged with emotions. But if the book is never written and published, it becomes one's incompletion. Also recorded as incompletions are the memories of hurts that you pushed from your conscious Mind (called "repressions.") You believe you got rid of them, but they are alive and well in your Unconscious and now push around your decisions. Your Unconscious also registers as incompletions:

⇒ decisions by default, i.e., the decisions you needed to make, but did not
⇒ your unkind acts toward self and others
⇒ unresolved conflicts
⇒ patterns of behavior that throw you out of balance

How do you know what your incompletions are? Your Unconscious knows and it pulls you into the situations that give you a chance to *complete, i.e., to handle your challenge without going out of balance*. Have you noticed that you tend to be confronted with the same issues and similar situations over and over? That is not accidental. Every situation, including the one you are in right now, offers you opportunities to complete some of your incompletions. Moreover, your Unconscious may elicit particular reactions from others to create a chance for you to complete. For example, unable to face conflicts, Maurice would run away from them. The inability to live his truth was his incompletion. He kept finding himself in one conflict after another until it dawned on him to learn to stand his ground. He began learning with gusto whatever could help him – from negotiation skills to martial arts. That is a wise approach.

> *Once you complete an incompletion, i.e., once it stops being an issue within you, the outer world responds in kind. It does not confront you with that issue anymore.*

137

How the hooks of the past derail your current decisions.

Have you ever reacted to someone's words or behavior in a way that surprised yourself and that canceled an opportunity that seemed custom-made for you? Such strong – "out-of-proportion" -- reactions usually stem from old hurts or other incompletions, stored in the unconscious. Each incompletion paves the way for more incompletions. That is how the unconscious operates, and no human being, however rich, brilliant, educated or spiritual, is exempt. The story of my client Ann illustrates how an old hurt brings forth more hurts. Ann was enthusiastic about a chance to become an accountant for a big company. Yet, during the interview for the job, she found herself inexplicably abrasive toward the interviewer, who, Ann admitted, had done nothing wrong. An explanation came weeks later when Ann stumbled over an old photo album in her attic. A picture there cut open an old agony. The picture was of her ex-husband Steve, whom Ann had adored and who had left Ann ten years ago for her closest friend Angela. Ann felt now, as she felt then, a pain so sharp, it was as if she were being stabbed slowly with a poisoned dagger. She did not remember how long she sat in the attic. Then something prompted her to look at that picture again. In it, Steve, dressed in his usual aristocratic manner, was wearing an expensive ivory colored shirt embossed with a particular pattern. Where had Ann seen this pattern recently? Oh, God, that interviewer's tie had had the same pattern! Ann had no conscious memory of the pattern on Steve's shirt. The memory was buried in her unconscious, along with her unbearable anguish over feeling betrayed and rejected by her husband and closest friend -- the two people she had loved and trusted most. Unknown to Ann, that old hurt had made her abrasive during the interview, assuring another rejection. If Ann does not heal this hurt, it will create more hurts.

The unconscious operates as if each incompletion were a hook that drags down whatever is associated with it. These hooks form a wheel that keeps turning as we move through life. As the wheel is turning, each hook takes hold of new incompletions, which become new hooks, seizing, grabbing, and catching more hooks (1). With more new hooks gripped, old hooks grow into clusters. This means incompletions pile up in our lives, and we find ourselves entangled in loose ends. Then we become indecisive; 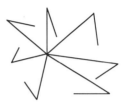 our resistance to change grows, and it takes us longer to accept the new. Mentally and emotionally, we resist everything that differs from our routine. The piling up of incompletions results in lack of energy and enthusiasm. Physically, incompletions are reflected in excess weight, constipation, muscle tensions, clutter in our files, closets, drawers, disc storages, garages. Emotionally, we grow more irritable, resentful, moody, frustrated. Mentally, we find ourselves foggy, confused, scattered, needing more time "to sort things out." We spend more and more time on relationships and activities that only add more junk and clutter to our lives.

Each hook represents an incompletion. Each hook also represents the energy you have put into an incomplete project -- into that boat you began to build, into an old hurt. This energy, hooked in your Unconscious, becomes unavailable to you. The more hurts and incompletions you pile up, the more energy you lock in your Unconscious. Then comes fatigue: "Oh, I have no energy to decide anything, let alone follow through with my decisions." What is the way out then? The way out goes through "undoing" the cause, i.e., through completing.

By completing you reclaim energy from your Unconscious.

139

Chapter 7

Ways to Free Yourself from Your Past

Safe techniques to clear old hurts.

Many incompletions are old hurts. To explain how to heal them I will use the case of a 43-year-old Kevin, who volunteered to share his old hurt with the group in a decision- making training I conducted. Kevin told us: "When I was in high school, I badly wanted to date Sue, a tall slender blonde. Finally, I got a date with her, but later I learned that I got it because someone else had broken a date and she was stuck for the night. It hurt me so badly that I wanted to kill myself. I got over it, but at the oddest times this hurt still bothers me."

One technique is simply to *acknowledge that right now your old hurt has no physical reality. None whatsoever.* Kevin's hurt occurred more than twenty years ago, and for all those years he used his Imagination to re-create the hurt and feed it with the energies of his Mind and Emotions. The realization of how you yourself perpetuate the hurt may clear the hurt.

CLEAR AN OLD HURT

> ➤ Think of a hurt you would like to clear
> ➤ Relax. You may put soft music on and make yourself comfortable in a chair or on the floor. Close your eyes, uncross your legs and arms and observe your breathing until relaxation takes place
> ➤ Realize that the situation where the hurt occurred is not present anymore. It is alive only in your memory. Each time you recalled it in your Imagination you yourself were making sure that the hurt would not go away. You fed it with the energy of your own thoughts and feelings
> ➤ Right now choose to stop feeding the hurt. If you do,
> ➤ You feel your energy increased – you've reclaimed the energy that was tied with this hurt in your Unconscious

➢ Mentally direct the freed energy to your current project and immediately start physically working on the project.

➢ When using this and the following techniques, have your Imagination fill, surround, and protect you and the people connected to your old hurt with pure white light, which is known to increase clarity and peace.

> *For your Unconscious the events you imagine are as real as those which take place physically.*

So, another clearing technique involves making up a new – happy – ending to the situation where your hurt occurred.
Here is how it worked for Kevin.

K: I want Sue to become fat and ugly. That would bring me real satisfaction!

A: Putting down or hurting anyone, even in your Imagination, does not heal. We heal an old hurt with a happy ending for both parties.

K: Then a happy ending for me would be this. We both have a great time that evening, the time of our lives. We really come to appreciate each other.

A: OK, Kevin, relax. Fill and surround yourself and Sue with white light. Let your Imagination create your great evening with Sue. Make it as beautiful as you can. See her beauty, see yourself looking irresistibly attractive, hear her laughing at your jokes, smell the fragrances of the evening, sense the silk of her skin. Fill in any details you wish. It is your scenario. Take her to a royal palace if you wish. The more alive and delightful you make your evening with Sue the more thorough is the clearing... How do you like it?

K: Wow, it's great.

A: Dwell there for a while.

Chapter 7

If the imaginary experience is strong, the clearing may occur the first time. Sometimes, however, you will need to apply the techniques more than once. As you experience the peace and joy of the happy ending in your Imagination, the levels below the conscious accept this ending as real, and a healing of memory occurs. Note: To clear a hurt, just reading about the techniques is not enough. You need to apply them.

> *What tells you that you have cleared a hurt? The memory of the event loses its emotional charge.*

The event may never pop into your memory again. By the same token, recurring memories of people or episodes you'd rather skip, usually signal old hurts you need to heal.

The clearing of one incompletion may dissolve an entire cluster of incompletions, freeing areas of life you never knew were tied to that old hurt or incompletion. Kevin, who bravely volunteered to clear his hurt in front of the group, told us how he was rewarded beyond his expectations. Kevin is a Vietnam War veteran. For five years he was grappling with his war issues in psychotherapy, yet the memories of war still disturbed him so much that he wouldn't want even to pass by a movie theater showing a film about Vietnam. The weekend after Kevin cleared his school hurt, he had a visit from Ron, with whom Kevin had served in the Marine Corps. Kevin told us, "As we were recalling the war, we both became incredibly nervous. Our bodies began to twitch, twist, and shake. At that point, I reminded myself that there was no reality to those old hurts anymore. That war couldn't hurt me now. I was safe. Ron and I unearthed issues and memories you wouldn't think could be of any use. Yet bringing them out in the open was like flushing them down the toilet. Now I can discuss Vietnam and feel relaxed. It is no longer an issue I am forcing down, fearing it will rise up and bother me again. I addressed those memories and flushed them away." Kevin and Ron ended up watching a movie about Vietnam, having a good time and even laughing.

Your Unconscious and Emotions don't relate to time as your Mind does. A hurt experienced by a two-year-old causes pain to an adult twenty years later, although the Mind erased its memory. But once a hurt is healed, it is healed completely despite all the times you endured it.

As we clear some hurts, others surface -- the ones we had forgotten, the ones we did not know existed. It is like cleaning a dirty room. As the obvious dirt gets cleaned out, we uncover stains that were covered with dust before.

Other ways to free yourself from your past.

> *To free yourself from your past you need to complete what you set in motion.*

There are two ways to complete. One way is to finish a decision, i.e., to bring it to an end physically and then let go of thoughts, feelings, and everything else related to this project. The other way applies when you abort a project without finishing it physically. You still must let go of thoughts, feelings, images, memories and everything else related to this project. Often, physical actions of finishing a decision use up the energies of negative emotions. Then it becomes easier to complete. Otherwise, we might have turned those energies against ourselves. Here is an example.

In 1987 Gary Hart, the leading candidate for the Democratic presidential nomination, dropped out of the campaign following the sensation over his involvement with a model, Donna Rice. He chose to finish physically his decision to run for President by reentering the campaign. At the time, his case was making the rounds among the comedians. To withstand the media scrutiny he needed a new strength. To gain it, Hart completed the Donna Rice episode. He went over it with his wife and children and reached the agreements that aligned his family behind him. (Completion always rewards!) After reentering the race, Hart received few votes. He lost that round of the Game. Was it a mistake on his part to reenter the campaign? Not at all. It is easier to complete a decision after we have physically exhausted our favorite option. Besides, to become true winners in the Game of Life we must learn to lose graciously. And how can we learn without practicing?

Hart could have chosen to complete differently. After the Donna Rice episode, he could have dropped his goal to become President and -- in the privacy of his inner decision team – let go of everything related to that goal. Right then, he could have charted for himself a new course in life. However, he was not ready to let go, and the completion within your own team works *only if you truly let go.* If you declare that you are done with a project or a relationship but resist parting with any material possessions, feelings, images, or thoughts related to that project or relationship, you have lied to yourself. You have not let it go. What is holding you back? Hopes of returning to it? Unacknowledged attachments? Those are incompletions! If they are not cleared out, they will drain your energy and push your decisions around. Then you might experience depression, stagnation, financial losses, or diseases – those are the high price we pay for holding on inwardly to the corpses of the past.

When our "unfinished business" involves other people, it is preferable to "clear the air" through personal interactions. However, the completing can be done unilaterally, inwardly.

> *If you reached peace inside in regard to a disturbing or horrible past experience, if you truly forgave yourself and those involved, you completed that episode whether or not others forgave and completed.*

Again, it works only if we have truly manage to forgive. If you find it hard to forgive yourself or someone else, reread the section "Emotional Traps" in Chapter 5.

This may surprise you: *if you are an active decision-maker, pleasant memories must go as well.* Why? Because memories belong to the past game, and they distract your players from winning now. However cozy and comfortable the cocoon, it has to go entirely, or no butterfly can come into being. Do not be concerned about holding on to the past. The Universe is rich beyond our Imagination; the Universe is eager to give. What happened five minutes ago is already a memory. Each day is a new day. Each hour is a new hour. Each moment is a new moment. That is freedom!

How to increase your energy anytime.

Do you want to increase your energy level? Complete a few incompletions. With each completion, you will gain the energy that was locked in your Unconscious. How do you know that more energy has become available? Fatigue vanishes. Whereas before you needed ten hours of sleep daily, now you find that six hours is plenty. You'll experience well-being.

Do you feel stuck in your current decision? Complete an incompletion and watch how your energy and ingenuity become available for your current decision.

To prevent new incompletions be vigilant. How? By committing only to what you truly want to complete. When you say, "I am going to do this," your Unconscious assigns energy to this project. You may forget that you intended to do that

145

project, but your Unconscious, whose job is to record your experiences, keeps the energy assigned for that project stored away. That energy becomes unavailable for anything else. In other words, by starting and not completing, you create a hidden drainage of your energies. So next time, before saying, "I am going to...," ask yourself whether you are really committed. If you feel committed but later reconsider and want to abort a project, let your Unconscious know that. How? Simply by affirming to yourself that you are dropping the project and making sure that all your players let the project go. To avoid creating new incompletions vigilance becomes the order of the day.

Your opportunities to break free.

It can be very painful to touch an old hurt hidden in the Unconscious. It is also such a relief to heal old hurts. So you want to be gentle with yourself yet firm. When you come close to clearing a hook, be it an old hurt or another incompletion, your Unconscious puts up various defenses. Your energy gets drained into your Unconscious, i.e., you start going unconscious: yawning, nodding, spacing-out, feeling tired and drowsy. Or, you want to get up and leave. Or, you start feeling scared. Or you get angry, resentful and start judging the people involved so you can righteously avoid facing and clearing your incompletions.

Your Unconscious may distract you in various other ways. Self-pity with its whining tune, "Poor me... poor me" may drive you into overeating, smoking, sex, talk, alcohol, all of which consume the time and energy you need for completing. You may feel a "noble" urge to fix someone else's life at the expense of freeing yourself by completing what you had started. When the time comes to let go of your mental-emotional attachments and material possessions, the emotions of Panic and Distrust bring forth Insecurity. It screams and clings to relationships, jobs, and places that no longer hold any promise for you. Insecurity clings to them as if they could secure your freedom. But *true freedom and wealth are measured not by what you have, but by what you can do without.*

At first, various defenses of your Unconscious deter you. But gradually you grow able to recognize them. That grants you a choice. You can either succumb to unconscious energies or gain strength and pass through the unconscious defenses. If you choose to pass, you may remind yourself, "If my Unconscious is putting up defenses, I must be close to completing something important. Right now is my moment of opportunity!" To gain strength to complete, some people pray, others enlist friends' help, still others promise themselves a reward – a vacation, a good movie, etc. Do whatever inspires you and adds strength to complete.

If you've gotten the impression that your Unconscious is harsh, answer this: Do you want to keep your decision-making weaknesses hidden (even from yourself)? Do you want them to lead you astray at a trying moment, or would you rather have them surface so you can replace them with strengths? It is a vital job of your Unconscious to test if you are strong enough for the next level of freedom. Completing makes you ready for the next rounds in your Game of Life.

The name of the crowning decision-making phase is not "perfection" but "completion." Complete the best you can now and you are free!

Tomorrow or in ten days you may be able to complete better. Yet, by completing now you free yourself to enter a new, more exciting game NOW. We win the Game of Life by continually completing, by letting go. So let go of your past with joy. Make the letting go a celebration. It is. It clears the room for the fathomless riches of the Universe to enter your life.

Mirrors That Help Make Instant Decisions

Do you know that the mirrors of your Unconscious are always here for you? They reflect to you – instantly -- how you go about your decisions and how you can do better. Where are they? Everywhere. Symbolically, everything and everyone reflects you back to you. At first, interpretations of this symbolic language may seem far-fetched or even silly. But as you gain fluency in the native tongue of your Unconscious, you come to appreciate its depth of meaning, economy of form and the priceless decision clues it delivers. Out of countless mirrors of the unconscious, we will look into a few.

MIRROR #1

The world around you mirrors the issues you have. When they stop being issues, in other words, when something that used to disturb you no longer does, the outer world, as if by magic, stops confronting you with that issue. My client, Timothy, has experienced that recently. A devoted family man, he loves going out with his old buddies once a month. They meet on the last Tuesday, and as the time draws near Timothy cringes, knowing that his wife, Dorothy, will make a scene about his outing. Once Timothy's friend Mel asked why Timothy felt so guilty about his outings.

T: There is always so much to do for the kids.

M: But you keep coming here.

T: I love it here. Here I'm part of Jack's band, of Paul's police patrol, of Jim's school, of your auto shop, of Rick's crazy business. We've always been there for each other.

M: We need our gatherings. Can't Dorothy get it?

T: I guess it's me. I feel guilty for taking the time out.

M: I think we ought to give ourselves a break. If we don't, we'll explode, start resenting our families and taking it out on the kids.

It made sense, and Timothy relaxed about the outings. Soon Dorothy told him she had signed up for a class that met on Tuesday evenings and arranged for a baby-sitter. "Do you mind, Tim?" Timothy did not mind at all. That is how it works. Once his outings stopped being an issue for Timothy, Dorothy's monthly scenes became history.

MIRROR # 2

Observe how you approach meals (at home, in a restaurant, at a picnic, wherever) and jot down your observations
➢ Notice how the way you approach your meals mirrors symbolically the way you approach decisions
➢ Record insights in your journal
➢ How can you use these insights to improve your decision-making?

E.g., Kim comments, "There are so few foods I can eat." The same way she limits herself in decisions. Her constant refrain is, "I have no choice!" In fact, she has many choices. Kim needs to focus on discovering many options she actually has.

MIRROR # 3

➢ Think of your current problem
➢ While focusing on it, get up and start walking
➢ Observe how you walk while thinking of your problem
➢ How does the way you walk reflect how you go about this problem

Lori observes that when she's preoccupied with her problem, her walk becomes heavy, her weight falls primarily on her heels. She uses only part of her feet. That throws her off-balance, pulling her back. Lori comments, "My past is holding me back from dealing with this problem."

║➤ How can you benefit from the insights you've got ?
Lori's answer: "I can change my attitude. I'm taking a full breath, focusing on peace, on my son's smile. As I walk, I use my feet fully and my weight creates a forward momentum. My problem no longer saddles me. I can handle it."

MIRROR # 4

What improvement does each of these people need most:

║➤ your spouse
║➤ your child
║➤ your parents
║➤ your boss
║➤ your subordinates
║➤ your partner or coworker
║➤ your friend
║➤ the President of the United States?

Jot down your answers right away, before reading any further.

Guess who needs most what you jotted down for them? YOU!

DISCOVER YOUR NEXT STEP

║➤ Choose a person about whom you care most
║➤ What do you criticize about him/her most?
║➤ Pay attention to the advice you've given them. It mirrors-- directly or symbolically -- what <u>you</u> need to do, i.e., your next step. Turn the energy you put into fixing his/her life toward fixing your own.

MIRROR #5

Dreams are, indeed, your "magic mirror" (2). When your Body rests and your conscious Mind releases its grasp, your

Unconscious takes over and, with active help from your Coach, helps you *rehearse all major decisions of your life*. It certainly pays to learn interpreting your dreams.

All mirrors of the Unconscious reflect what we create. The Unconscious implements a universal law: each creation returns to its creator. We can move away from our creations physically, forget them mentally, and repress the emotions related to them, but we cannot bribe the Unconscious. It records whatever we create -- mess, hurt, goodness -- and then pulls us into situations where we receive what we created -- mess, hurt, goodness. Finally, it dawns on us that if we want joy, freedom, and peace, we must make decisions that create joy, freedom, and peace. All in all, the Unconscious strengthens us into loving ourselves enough to receive the very best through giving our very best. Isn't it amazing how we resist accepting this deal?

The Universe mirrors us back to ourselves, but for a long time we keep disowning our reflections. When we own them, we learn to complete out of love and respect for self and others. It is a beautiful time -- the time of healing old wounds and hurts, the time of cleaning out inner and outer clutter. It is a time that can lead to serenity and joy. Some people put off the clearing of their unconscious till they are on their death bed. If they're lucky, they may die free. The other decision -- to live free -- entails the clearing of your Unconscious now.

How to prevent creating more hooks to the past.

We create more hooks when our incompletions pile up. My client, Clayton, put it this way, "I am caught in a net of loose ends. I tie up one, trip over another, and another, and still another one. There seems to be no end to them. I feel so overwhelmed I end up doing nothing and feeling ashamed of myself. Then I go to my fridge and I eat ..." Sound familiar? To dissolve loose ends and prevent creating more of them we need to discover our true priorities and then stick to them.

HOW TO PRIORITIZE IN A HURRY

The following exercise, offered in awareness trainings, clarifies priorities in a hurry. Let's pretend that:

> ➤ You have only one hour left to live.
> ➤ What must be handled within this hour?
> ➤ What will be your top priority?
> ➤ Now you are given a day to live.
> ➤ What is most important for you to handle in this day?
> ➤ Now you have a month to live.
> ➤ What comes first now?
> ➤ Now six months...

In the last moments before death our disagreements, irritations, and resentments become insignificant. What comes to the fore is the pure true loving that is a basic need of every human being. Loving is all that counts. Everything else becomes immaterial. A single priority stands out above all -- to communicate our love and appreciation to ourselves, to our children, parents, spouses, friends. Whether we are to live 60 seconds or 60 years more, the top priority for each moment is to deepen our loving. If we stick to this one priority in each decision we make, we have absolutely won the Game of Life.

Unconditional loving heals the deepest hurts and produces the fastest completion. Boundless new vistas open. It is as though we lived in a cave sealed with a huge rock. The rock is removed. We stand up in the peaceful shining daylight, and the whole universe welcomes us free.

Completion is the most magical phase in decision-making, because completion sets you free.

Summary

Everything and everyone reflects you back to you. Use symbolic mirrors of your Unconscious to get instant clues for decisions and set yourself free by completing.

YOUR UNCONSCIOUS,
THE MOST INFLUENTIAL PLAYER ON YOUR DECISION TEAM

HIGH PRODUCTIVITY

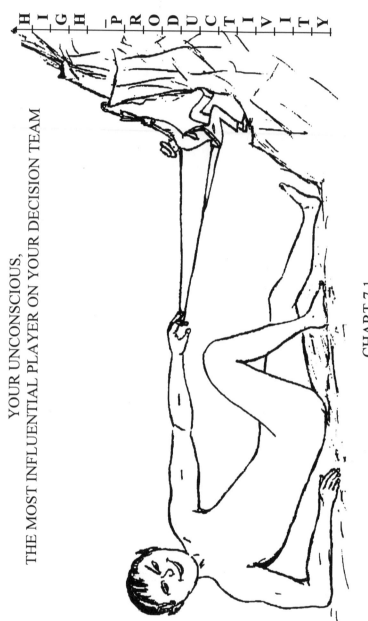

CHART 7.1

8

Your Intuition

In this chapter you will learn how to align with your Coach, sensitize yourself to intuition and build your intuitive powers.

How Great People Arrive at Great Decisions

You have come to the most precious dimension of your inner compass – your Coach, your intuition.

> *According to Webster's, intuition is an immediate knowing without reasoning. The Encyclopedia Britannica defines intuition as an original, independent source of knowledge that accounts for the kinds of knowledge other sources do not provide.*

Here is an example. In Washington, D.C., a 10-minute walk from the White House, there sits a statue of Samuel Hahnemann, a German physician whose intuition gave us homeopathy. Hahnemann was a medical doctor, and as such he prescribed drugs to his patients to eliminate undesirable symptoms. But the side effects of the drugs concerned him so much that he undertook extensive research that led him to this revelation. Disease symptoms are the body's attempts to rid itself of the disease. The physician can amplify the body's healing powers by giving the patient tiny doses of the remedies that cause the symptoms of the disease being treated. For instance, belladonna in large doses causes a sore throat in healthy people, but in tiny doses it cures sore throat. The principle of like curing like was not predictable from the standpoint of traditional medicine (1,2.)

Intuition is the language of your Coach. As was mentioned in chapter 2, all decision-making messages come from your players and your Coach. While no player is fully aware of the other members on your team and no player is aware of the entire field, your Coach is. From outside of the field the Coach can see the vistas related to your decision. That is why intuition brings a higher knowing no other source can provide, as this real-life story illustrates.

1971. An affluent New Jersey town. The police opened the grand Victorian mansion of the List family and walked into a horror movie. Four corpses on the floor and a fifth one stuffed in the third floor closet had been decaying there for a month. The stereo was playing Bach's religious music. Placed next to the corpses was a note where List told his minister about murdering his wife, mother, and three children. List himself vanished. 1989. A bust of List, as he would look now, was shown on the "America's Most Wanted" TV show. The resemblance was such that the FBI arrested List within days. The bust was created by Frank Bender – without computers -- from an 18-year-old photo. A Philadelphia expert on forensic sculpturing, Bender gathered whatever information about List there was available, then let his intuition take over (3).

In a sense, making decisions is like driving. When you find yourself in traffic that crawls, should you take the first available exit or are you better off exercising patience and crawling with the traffic? A glance from a helicopter would let you know what is hidden from the drivers on the ground -- the overall flow of the traffic and thus what lies ahead. Intuition offers a bird's-eye view of decisions in their context -- hence, foresight.

Making a tough decision without intuition is like groping in a dark unfamiliar house where a time bomb may explode at any moment. Anxious to get out, you bump into things, break fragile souvenirs and cut your hands while moving pieces out of the way. For an instant, a bright light flashes, and you see -- with utmost clarity -- how to exit. This is what intuition does in decisions -- it turns on a bright light.

How then can you turn on the light of your intuition? Answers can be found in famous intuitive decisions. Their brilliance may create the impression that intuition is a supernatural phenomenon, reserved for the greatest. It is not. Everyone has the capacity for instantaneous knowing.

You may ask, " If intuition is so great, why don't we receive it all the time?" We do not, because we cannot. Your Coach is happy to give it, but giving is a two-way process – your players must be ready to receive. Intuition offers a spectacular panoramic view from the mountain top, but to receive it you must have climbed there. So let us explore how to do that.

Throughout history, great people have described how they arrived at their famous decisions. Although made in dissimilar eras, cultures, and walks of life, their descriptions contain -- with consistency -- these four steps: *preparation, incubation, illumination, and verification*, described by a French mathematician and philosopher, Poincare. He decided to prove that certain mathematical functions could not exist. After his intense efforts to disprove their existence failed, he thought that, after all, they existed. Yet, however he tried, he couldn't prove their existence either (preparation). So he left for a geological expedition that required his full attention (incubation). There, one day it dawned on him how to prove the existence of those functions (illumination). Later, he verified the existence of what he named "Fucksian functions," now much used in mathematics (4).

If you grasp how preparation and incubation work, you can use them at will to receive intuition. We examine the preparation first.

How to Make Your Breakthrough Inevitable

Good mountain climbers drop all weight and issues unrelated to reaching the top. Similarly, great decision-makers drop everything unrelated to their decision. Preparatory step may challenge you to the limit. Laced with obstacles, it is nevertheless enticing and romantic, for each move, each moment may open you to knowing. During preparation, sharpen your focus, i.e., direct all your resources toward finding and/or implementing your decision. Involve all your players, cleansing, sensitizing and strengthening them in the process. For instance, ancient leaders used to fast during the preparatory step to sharpen their mental focus, cleanse the body and increase its sensitivity. Engage your Imagination (chapter 4). Have you experimented with becoming -- in your Imagination -- the one you are deciding on? For instance, a detective identifies with a criminal to anticipate his moves, a cancer researcher identifies with a malignancy to learn its patterns of growth, and parents identify with their kids to help them cope. Watch how your Emotions react to the issues in question. Feed on their energy and information (chapter 5). Make sure that your Mind supports you in all ways (chapter 6). Tie up loose ends, and use the mirrors of your Unconscious (chapter 7).

Anyone studying famous decisions can't help but notice that great decision-makers do the preparation phase with gusto. By doing their "homework" enthusiastically and thoroughly they lay out the foundation for greatness.

Here is Sir Alec Guinness, a famous British actor, who created over a hundred dissimilar characters, including an Arab prince, two women, a Chinese cook, Hamlet, Hitler, Shylock, Obi-Wan Kenobi, and even a wolf. A chameleon extraordinaire, he played eight roles in one comedy. For Guinness, preparation for the decision of how to play a new role started with learning how his character walks. He would search the streets for someone who looked right for his character, then follow the person, imitating his walk, gestures, facial expressions and way of talking. Having *emptied himself of everything unrelated to his decision* of how to play his new role, he'd perfect his mimicry until he knew intuitively how his character felt inside (5,6).

➤ Have you prepared for your current decision thoroughly and with gusto?

If a decision does not come, how long should you remain in the preparatory step? When should you move to incubation? Here is a tip. Pinpoint the one thing that, in your perception, holds you back. If you have a few such things, it usually spells, "Back to the drawing board. You have not finished your preparation." Example. Frank Bender had to find the answers to many questions. How would a scar from surgery List had had on his skull change List's face 18 years later? For answers Bender contacted the University of Pennsylvania. To discuss List's character and motives, Bender met with a Michigan expert on criminal profiling. Bender searched out information on List's eating habits, on how List walked, and much more.

Chapter 8

Bender moved to incubation when only the question about the expression of List's eyes was left unanswered.

If you tend to overstay in preparation, you waste time and effort. What do you risk by ending preparation prematurely? Not much. Your incubation will not result in illumination, so you will have to do more homework. That's all. So, experiment with ending preparation earlier than you used to, trusting that your Unconscious and Coach will make their contributions.

> In your current decision, what (if anything) do you need to do to finish preparation and shift to incubation?

Incubation -- a technique for arriving at great decisions.

During preparation you create a vortex of energy to "suck in" intuition. But emotional pressures and mental limitations during decision-making may prevent you from receiving intuition. Incubation refocuses your Mind and Emotions and lets your Unconscious and Coach piece together bits of the puzzle and add new knowing. Those dynamics are illustrated by a charming story, told to the Royal Society of London by a famous German chemist, August Kekule, who discovered the structure of benzene, the basis of a great many organic compounds. While researching that structure, one night Kekule was nodding in front of his fireplace. There he saw the atoms of a benzene molecule dancing before his eyes, twining and twirling like a snake. Suddenly, the snake seized its tail, closing the circle. Wow! Here was his decision -- the molecule of benzene was a closed ring! It was a very daring idea. At that time, chemists did not know of any ring-shaped molecules. Nor did they know a type of chemical bond that could support this idea. Kekule intuited a new, special type of chemical bond that makes benzene such an exceptionally stable compound (7).

Many great decisions have been incubated in the dream state.

USE NIGHT SLEEP (OR DAY-TIME NAP) TO INCUBATE A DECISION

➤ Eat lightly or fast during the day and stay away from consciousness-altering drugs and alcohol
➤ Before falling asleep:

    a/ focus on the goal of your decision; make sure that no other thought competes for your attention; also ask that only that which is for the highest good of all concerned come forward

    b/ put a pad and a pen next to you to record the dream immediately

    c/ imagine how you will feel when the decision comes; luxuriate in that feeling -- joy, relief, gratitude, whatever it is

    d/ ask your Unconscious and Coach to reveal to you a decision in a dream that you can understand

Silence is also a great incubator of intuition. A rather extreme example of that comes from Russian art history. Andrei Rublyov, a great Russian artist, chose to stop talking after he lost a woman he loved to a violent crowd. Seven silent years later, Rublyov reappeared as a genius of the pre-Renaissance period. The famous icons he created convey an enormous power of spirit. To get in touch with your inner stillness so that the Mind's chatter does not shatter your inner silence, you may want to practice spiritual exercises (8).

How have other famous people incubated their decisions? Poincare went on a geological excursion. Einstein resorted to playing the violin. Christian Dior gardened and made liqueur from the berries in his garden. Isaac Asimov, a Nobel Prize winner and science fiction writer, watched action movies until – without thinking about it – he'd have his answer (9). The illustrations at the end of this chapter show some other ways to incubate. The trick is to *shift your focus away from your decision to something that entirely consumes your attention.* Incubate your decisions by doing what you really like, as great people do.

Can you quicken incubation? You can if you've completed your preparation, give incubation all your attention and are open to intuition. With those prerequisites, you can incubate a decision, for instance, through:
⇒ focusing on breathing
⇒ taking a shower or bubble bath
⇒ moving to observation
⇒ changing your attitude
⇒ meditating or doing spiritual exercises (8)

Breakthrough.

The next step is often called "eureka" in honor of what occurred in the prosperous city of Syracuse about 250 B.C. King Hiero II of Syracuse had ordered his new crown to be made of pure gold. But what if a cheaper metal had been added? His royalty abhorred being cheated. So he charged his famous subject Archimedes with finding out. It was easy to calculate the volume of the crown by dividing its weight by the density of gold. If copper or silver were added, they would increase the volume, since they are less dense than gold. But how do you measure the actual volume of the crown?! After struggling with that task for a while, Archimedes gave himself a break. He went to a public bath where in those times the life-loving Greeks received massages, exercised, discussed the news and otherwise socialized. Apparently, the attendant filled the bath to the rim. When Archimedes got in, water spilled over. At that instant, it dawned on him that the volume of the spilled water equaled the volume of his body. Of course, the crown would also displace the amount of liquid equal to its volume. The brilliant simplicity of the decision made the famous Greek forget his attire and run home, shouting ecstatically, "Eureka! Eureka!" which is Greek for, "I found it! I found it!" They say that the ancient Greeks were more impressed with Archimedes's discovery than with the fact that the great man didn't bother to put on his toga or trunks. By the way, the crown proved to be an alloy (9).

Measured in clock time, the reception of intuitive messages may last a fraction of a second or much longer. But time is irrelevant when we touch eternity. And during eureka we do. Good descriptions of the eureka experience do not exist. How can they? One instrument cannot play a symphony. One player, the mind, however sharp and sophisticated, cannot convey the richest interplay of the entire team. Yet verbal descriptions, although inadequate, serve us. If nothing else, they inspire and create a longing for eureka. So here is how a scientist describes his eureka experience. "I was carried beyond pleasure.... My success...seemed insignificant beside this tranquil ecstasy. It was as though I...had become for a moment a part of the truth I sought, as though all the world, the atoms, and the stars were wonderfully clear and close to me, and I to them, so that we were part of a lucidity more tremendous than any mystery. I had never known that such a moment could exist.... I used to sneer at the mystics who have described the experience of being at one with God and part of the unity of things. After that afternoon ...I thought I knew what they meant (10)."

In such timeless moments of oneness with the universe a grand design may reveal itself and previously hidden correlations become apparent to you. You gain a sense of perfect well-being and the astounding clarity of knowing, "This is the way to go." Much more often, though, intuitive messages appear in the modest form of a flash, a picture, an image, a feeling, a knowing, a voice.

Risks and Safeguards of Acting on Intuition

Verification occurs when you act on intuition. For Frank Bender, for instance, verification came when List's picture taken at the time of his arrest proved practically identical to the picture of the bust Frank created. Basing decisions on intuition implies trusting it. When you follow intuition, you develop a relationship with it. Each time you act on your intuition, you build your intuitive powers; each time you ignore intuition, you deaden your ability to receive intuition. If you do not apply the intuitive knowing received, intuition does not frequent you anymore.

➤ Do you act on your intuition?
➤ What have your most recent intuitions and insights suggested?
➤ Have you acted on them fully or shrugged them off?

Mrs. Fields wanted to offer her cookies to the market, but marketing experts told her that the market had absolutely no room for another cookie shop. All her friends expressed the same opinion. She chose to act on her intuition. Several years later her cookie business topped $30 million in profits (11).

Often verification involves risk. Dr. Land, for instance, had to invest substantial resources to introduce his Polaroid camera to the market . To outsiders the risk may look huge, but the decision-maker himself or herself may not perceive his/her actions as that risky because intuition has revealed to him/her the inner connections of things.

There is a risk, however, of mistaking for intuition messages born out of our conditionings and desires, especially unconscious ones. No rule or instruction can fully guarantee that one identifies intuition correctly. Nevertheless, safeguards help.

SAFEGUARDS:

> ➤ Focus on your breathing until you feel relaxed
> ➤ Imagine implementing the message you received, whether it is intuition or not. While you are imagining:
>   a/ does your Body feel better?
>   b/ do you feel freer?
>   d/ do you feel more joyful?
>   e/ do you feel more peaceful?
> ➤ If you've received intuition, the answers will be "yes"
> ➤ Once you start acting on your intuitive leads, watch feedback. If you are in line with intuition, you are likely to feel a quiet or exuberant enthusiasm or other signs of connecting with your Coach

Intuitive messages may surprise or shock you. Yet, something inside, namely, your Coach, knows that they are true. Mary Kay's story illustrates the point. Mary Kay, who created a cosmetic product corporation, yielded to her pastor's request to speak at the church about their Sunday school fundraising. She had no time to prepare her speech, and on Sunday morning, while dressing hurriedly for church, she prayed to the Lord to fill her mouth with worthwhile words. Suddenly, a loud thought stopped her in her tracks: "Mary Kay, tell the congregation you'll match whatever they'll give today." So shocked was she, that she exclaimed out loud, "Wait just a minute, Lord! I've got to think this over!" When called to the pulpit, she heard herself saying that her foundation would match -- in cash -- this Sunday's donations. The audience did not seemed moved. After church nobody called, and she thought her speech had failed and they had collected so little that they were embarrassed to call. Indeed they were, but for a different reason. They had collected a phenomenal donation. Finally, the chairman of the building committee phoned to say that they had decided not to hold her to her offer to match, because nobody expected that much. Mary Kay got excited, thinking that they'd collected five or even ten thousand dollars. "How much?" she demanded. "$107,748." She grew silent. He repeated that she did not have to match it. Yet she knew that her guidance was to match the collection immediately and in cash. She said firmly that she would match. But how? She kept little in her savings account, investing money as it came. Where on earth could she get that much cash today? She prayed to know how to make good on her promise. Within minutes, the phone rang. It was her son Richard, who a while ago had persuaded her to invest in oil wells. She'd forgotten about it. Now he was excitedly telling her that their wells were gushing oil and this month her profits from them would exceed a hundred thousand dollars. Relieved and grateful, Mary Kay gave that money to the church (12).

Have you ever thought you acted on intuition, followed safeguards yet made a wrong decision? What caused that? Has an attachment to a specific outcome colored your perception? In any case, through this exercise benefit from your error.

BENEFIT FROM YOUR ERROR:

> Relax (for instance, by focusing on breathing)
> Watch the "movie" of your experience where you made an error
> Pinpoint where you went astray
> What warnings did you have but ignored?
> What inside you made you ignore the warnings?
> What will help you avoid similar errors in the future?
> Write answers in your journal

All in all, while basing your decisions on intuition involves risk, not following intuition guarantees that you will miss out on the very best in the Game of Life.

How to Increase Your Intuitive Powers.

First of all, how do you know whether your intuitive powers increase? They do
⇒   if you receive intuition ever more frequently,
⇒   if you can access intuition more quickly than before,
⇒   if the scope and depth of your intuition increase.

TO INCREASE YOUR INTUITIVE POWERS

➢ hold a clear intention to do that
➢ prepare and incubate the eureka experience as often as you can
➢ act on your intuition -- base on it your decisions
➢ use your mistakes to further your intuitive powers
➢ purge your players continually
➢ identify with your Coach

Purging Your Players

Your Coach's intuition can reach the Game field only by filtering through your players. The cleaner and healthier the players, the less they pollute intuitive messages. But if one's body is unhealthy, the imagination spins destructive fantasies, the mind dwells on negative thoughts, the emotions are in turmoil, and the unconscious is cluttered with incompletions, then intuitive messages -- if one gets them at all -- become distorted.

Purge your players continually. Cleanse and nourish, exercise and groom your Body, dwell on images of health and wealth, joy, and peace, take emotional showers frequently to

167

wash out negative emotions, tie up loose ends and, instead of thinking negatively, focus on your Coach.

As your players are purged, they fill up with the spirit of the Coach. Then your thoughts and emotions do not get sticky but rather pass through you like the shadows of airplanes over fields. You will have earned the viewer's seat for the divine comedy of life when you can, at your volition, zip in and out of your thoughts, emotions, and attachments as if they were clothes that you can change and discard. Note: the purging of the players is a lifetime job, because of the physical and psychic pollution around us.

Identifying with your Coach

When you identify with your Coach, you respond to life and its challenges as your Coach would. Let us look at examples.

Integrity There is the quality of integrity in Mary Kay's story recounted earlier. She could have skipped church that Sunday. Given her responsibilities as head of a Fortune 500 corporation, everyone would have understood. She chose to keep her commitment. She could have taken the chairman's offer not to match the funds. Given the phenomenal amount of donations, everyone would have understood. Instead, she chose to stick to what she knew as her truth. *Living a life of integrity opens one to intuition.*

Joy In the mid-seventies, the Soviet government threw human rights spokesman Nathan Sharansky in prison. Accused of spying for the US, he was held for nine years in freezing, windowless punishment cells, under the threat of execution. He was losing his eyesight and suffering chest pain. Yet, incredibly, Sharansky experienced profound joy. He found joy in remaining true to himself and in newly found spiritual oneness. He felt a spiritual bond with Socrates and Don Quixote, Ulysses and Hamlet. He felt that their struggles and laughter resonated with his own and that his decisions, like theirs, had the power to inspire or disenchant those who would come in the future. Through his joy and integrity, Sharansky was in touch with intuition.

The KGB (secret police) entirely deprived him of contacts with the outside world; his interrogators fed him clever lies. Yet, Sharansky appeared well informed about the developments outside his prison cell that related to him. The KGB furiously searched for his source of information. But the source – his intuition – was beyond their reach (13).

Sharansky's story is an inspiration and a real proof that there are no prerequisites for feeling joy. Being human is enough! Use the quiz at the end of this chapter to bring more joy into your life.

Inner Stillness Sir Alec Guinness had the "still center" that defied us "to will our eyes away. " (6) To maintain inner stillness Guinness lead an uncluttered life. His demeanor was described as unobtrusive and quiet, his looks as unmemorable. His hobby is fishing, and he lives with his wife in a modest house they built in southern England after World War II. Guinness made himself available to intuition and his intuition never let him down. Once, a young unknown director offered him a role. Guinness, then at the peak of his fame, did not like the science-fiction script and thought the dialogue appalling. But his intuition nudged him to meet the director. The young man offered Guinness a skimpy salary and two and a half percent of unknown future profits from the film. There seemed no good reason to accept the role, but his intuition prompted him to agree. The director was George Lucas. The film, "Star Wars," and its two sequels amassed well over $500,000,000 in the USA and Canada alone (5,6). To maintain the "still center" requires a strong commitment and daily practice (9). It also requires continuous vigilance, since each choice you make either distracts from or deepens your inner stillness.

<u>IDENTIFYING WITH YOUR COACH</u>

> ➤ What quality of your Coach would you like to master (stillness, humor, other – look at "Faces of the Coach" chart at the end of chapter 2)?
> ➤ Describe in your journal what you and your life would be like had you had that quality mastered
> ➤ What is the first step toward that mastery?
> ➤ View mastering that quality as upgrading your self-image and follow instructions for that in chapter 4

How to Prepare for the Unpredictable

You prepare for the unpredictable the same way you prepare to receive intuition. Indeed, nobody can predict when intuition will come (remember Archimedes, Poincare, Kekule, Mary Kay) or what the intuition will bring. To prepare for the unpredictable – and/or to receive intuition -- you want to be fluid and superflexible. Yet, our planet fosters ruts, addictions, routines and fossilized views that get in the way of intuition. To be prepared for the unpredictable, develop fluidity and keep sloughing off fixations, rigidity and stereotypes.

Fluidity. At the age of twelve, Bruce Lee, tired of being bullied at school, turned to martial arts for self-defense. Training under an old master, he practiced for hours with total devotion and never skipped his class. Yet, four years later mastery still eluded him. He was taught to avoid confrontation, but he'd be consumed with the thrust to beat his opponent and win. One day his master summed up for Bruce the principles of gaining control by swinging with the problem. Then he told Bruce to skip the class for a week. That week Bruce meditated for hours, then went sailing in a junk. On the sea, extremely angry with himself, he punched the water and, suddenly, became very still. He realized that the water had just illustrated the principle of martial arts that kept eluding him. When he struck with all his might, the water retreated, unhurt. He grasped it into his fist -- the water escaped. That was his instant of eureka. He felt one with nature. His entire decision team aligned with the fluidity of his Coach. He knew he would become like water (14).

DEVELOPING FLUIDITY AND SUPERFLEXIBILITY

> ➢ Experiment with the image of water:
> ➢ Identify with water. Imagine taking the shape of any container, then easily penetrating the hardest rock
> ➢ Under pressure (physical, emotional, mental), command yourself,
> ➢ "Become liquid!" Observe what happens
> ➢ Where in your current life do you need to be most fluid?
> ➢ In your Imagination experience yourself in that area as fluid and superflexible as you'd like to become

Drastic change in perspective may shatter the mind's rigidity and open one to eureka. When Edgar Mitchell walked on the moon, he was as pragmatic an engineer and scientist as one can be. But as his Apollo 14 was returning to Earth and he watched from outer space the majesty of our planet suspended as a precious "jewel against the black velvet of the sky," he experienced eureka. The presence of divinity became almost palpable to him and, in his words, "In one timeless moment I knew the Earth and its life were the result of an intelligent process." Mitchell thinks that anyone would experience intuition *when moved to a totally different perspective* (15, 16).

171

VIEW YOUR CURRENT DECISION FROM A DIFFERENT PERSPECTIVE

> ➤ Think of a person who, in your opinion, handles life superbly
> ➤ How would s/he decide in your situation?
> ➤ Look at your decision-making situation through the eyes of a Master. What decision would s/he make here? (17)
> ➤ What decision would you recommend if a friend were in your situation?
> ➤ In your Imagination become a wise being who loves you entirely and selflessly. What does s/he suggest that you do?
> ➤ What decision would your opponent suggest?
> ➤ Change your perspective drastically -- defend your opponent's point of view as if your life depended on it
> ➤ What insights have you gotten from this exercise?

SELF-QUIZ:

WHERE DO YOU STAND ON THE MISERY-JOY SCALE?

To bring more joy into your life, quiz yourself once a month. Enjoy lightening up and scoring better and better.

Key to Scoring:

yes – 10, no - 0,

never -- 0, rarely – 5, often - 10, usually -15, always - 20

On a scale where 10 is utmost bliss and 0 is utmost misery,

> ➤ where did you spend most of the last week? (That is your score)
> ➤ have you made a decision to focus on joy and keep yourself joyful? (You can make it now.)

➤ how do you cultivate joy in yourself and your life?
   Score 10 for each way in which you cultivate joy.

➤ When making a decision, do you take into account whether it will increase your joy? (never, rarely, often, usually, always)

➤ List three things that increase your joy
   a/ Do you have thing #1 in your life? (never, rarely, often, usually, always)
   b/ Do you have thing #2 in your life? (never, rarely, often, usually, always)
   c/ Do you have thing #3 in your life? (never, rarely, often, usually, always)

➤ Looking in the mirror, ask, "Am I joyful now?

➤ What would make me more joyful?" Let your team members one by one answer

➤ How have you responded to the answers: dismissed them /0/, put off considering them /5/, scheduled acting on them /15/, started acting on them /20/

➤ In what area of your life do you still feel dead serious?

➤ Despite the seriousness, do you sometimes feel joy in that area? (never, rarely, often, usually, always)

➤ What is your excuse for not feeling joy there? Remember: joy is determined not by circumstances but by your attitude

➤ Score 20 for turning your source of misery into a source of joy. Record in your journal how you did that

➤ Are you ready to bring joy into this area? How? Score 10 for each way that helps you find joy in this area
Two hints:1/ change your self-talk (what you tell yourself) and 2/ focus on what's joyful and funny

➤ Do you part more easily with joy /0/ or with misery /10/?

Have you noticed how your perspective can be changed by humor? If you have scored less than 205 in the above quiz, you may have contracted a debilitating disease scientifically termed "TYTS" -- Taking Yourself Too Seriously. It has killed more decision-makers than we can count. To cure TYTS, start awakening right away to ever present humor and joy. You are splendidly equipped to do that. Within you lives an Inner Humorist, a disguise of your Coach who does not get caught up in your problems, but reflects to you the divine comedy that your decision-making -- your Game of Life -- is.

Summary

Your Coach's intuition delivers foresight no player can provide. Do the preparation and incubation with gusto until you create your breakthrough. To receive more intuition, hold the receiving of intuition as your intention, purge your players, identify with your Coach, and use your mistakes to further your intuitive powers.

CHART 8.1

"I Love Change!"

CHART 9.1

9

Change: How to Spot New Opportunities

Decision-making always starts with change and results in more change. This chapter shows how to quicken your decision-making by quickening your response to change.

How to Quicken Your Response to Change

When Gladys returned home from work, she found a note from her husband Jim. The note informed her that he had left forever and did not want to be contacted. Gladys was so shocked, she could not even cry. "How come? I don't understand. So sudden..."

Was it, indeed, sudden? Gladys, have you forgotten how lost and desperate Jim looked when you said you never wanted children? Hadn't you noticed how he kept taking pictures of kids, how much he enjoyed children? In the last six months, didn't he come home late more and more often? And what about those uneasy feelings you have had around Jim lately?

No change is ever sudden.

> *You are forewarned about each substantial change. The signs of change are graded. As the red traffic lights appear only after the yellow lights have warned you, so in decision-making, at first, the "yellow light" warnings show up. If you miss or ignore them, the "red light" warnings appear, flashing and screaming for your attention.*

Each team member signals upcoming change in many ways. If you respond to the signals, you easily seize new opportunities.

What slows your response to change..

We humans have been slow to respond to change. Examples abound. Here is a dramatic one. Before the Holocaust, there was a short period when some of the Jews trapped in Nazi Germany might have escaped. But despite the Nazis' blatant anti-Semitism, the Jews kept hoping that the country they loved would wake up from the nightmare of fascism and treat them well. They ended up in concentration camps, having failed to recognize in time the need for a decision. They failed the beginning phase of decision-making.

Why are we slow to respond to change? First of all, because "inertia" is a fundamental trait of our planet. In physics, the very first law of motion is the law of inertia. It tells us that inertia causes matter at rest to resist movement and it causes moving matter to resist changing direction. Indeed, it takes force to get a truck moving, and when it moves, it takes force to change its direction.

Inertia is not limited to the realm of physics. Psychologically, inertia manifests as resistance to change. The fear of the new and the fear of change are instilled into us early in life. To protect children parents admonish, "Hold on to me. Don't go in the street! Don't eat what you don't know! Don't talk to strangers!" Since the child cannot gauge the speed of oncoming cars or differentiate between a healthy drink and liquid detergent, the parents' admonitions are warranted. But after we've grown up, those and similar admonitions sit in the unconscious as strong programming against newness and change. Then, like a heavy truck on the road, we keep the state we are in, clinging to familiar people, routes, and situations, even when it is painful.

The Lee Iacocca example is as good as any. When Iacocca was rising through the ranks of the Ford Motor Company, Henry Ford II considered Iacocca his protégé. After assuming presidency of the company in 1970, Iacocca noticed a change in Ford's attitude. In 1973 they had major disagreements. In 1975 Ford launched a full-scale investigation of Iacocca's business and personal life. It failed to produce damaging evidence but succeeded in turning Iacocca's life into hell. Yet, Iacocca stayed with the Ford Company until he was fired (1).

How could a man as dynamic and brilliant as Iacocca delay his response to change for over five years? Delay in responding to change is universal. Iacocca had worked for the Ford Motor Company for some 30 years and had never worked anywhere else. The inertia of familiarity was strong.

You cannot annul inertia. But you can reduce your resistance to change by choosing the right attitude toward change. There are two basic attitudes. You can view change as a menace and enemy, fear it, resist it and, as a result, develop diseases. Or, you can anticipate change and focus on the new opportunities change offers. Nobody is exempt from change. Change always wins, and those fighting change inevitably lose.

How can you quicken your response to change?

To answer, we break the beginning phase of multiphase decisions into four steps:

Chapter 9

1. Become aware of change
2. Accept the change (regard it as fact)
3. Sense if this change calls for a decision. If it does,
4. Refocus on a new direction

Let us take a closer look at each step.

Step 1: <u>Become aware of change</u>. In our two examples – the Jews in Germany and Iacocca – both were well aware of change. But it is not always the case. Take, for instance, Steve Jobs, the genius who cofounded Apple Computer. After he left Apple, Jobs and his staff, working day and night, created the great computer of the next generation. But Jobs overlooked a radical change in the marketplace — the introduction of Microsoft Windows. Inferior to Jobs' product but expertly marketed, Windows won the market, effectively closing opportunities for Job's product.

Step 2: <u>Accept change.</u> We will start exploring it with this example. On June 22, 1941 Nazi Germany "suddenly" attacked Russia. Joseph Stalin, then the absolute dictator of Russia, was so shocked that, uncharacteristically, he became unable to respond for two weeks. During those two weeks, Hitler occupied and ravaged one third of European Russia. Stalin called the attack sudden and perfidious, referring to the non-aggression pact Germany and Russia had recently signed. Yet, for years, top Soviet spies in Germany and Japan kept warning Moscow of Hitler's preparations to attack Russia. Winston Churchill, then Prime Minister of Great Britain, had warned Stalin that, according to British intelligence, a German attack on Russia was imminent. Moreover, huge German armies had been moved to Soviet borders months before the attack. Stalin responded with, "The Germans are just testing our nerves, and we have strong nerves." He forbade Soviet troops to respond to what he called

"German provocation." Whoever disobeyed was shot by Soviet military tribunals. For two weeks after the Nazis bombed Soviet territory, advanced far into it, devastating all in their path, Stalin's order forbidding the army to fight back was still in effect.

Stalin's unwillingness to accept the change — the fact that World War II had engulfed Russia -- appears grotesque. Yet, the truly grotesque thing is the awesome power Stalin wielded. The utmost unwillingness to accept change is common.

> *Accepting a change does not mean liking this change. It means simply recognizing what has already taken place.*

In other words, accepting change requires acknowledging change and acting on that knowledge rather than hoping that it will go away and "things will get back to normal."

Step 3: Discern whether this change calls for a decision Is this change of little consequence or does it start a new trend, a new direction, important and influential? Is it a trend of the future or a flash-in-the-pan? In retrospect, the answer seems obvious. But at the time it may not look obvious at all. When sound movies were introduced, many were convinced that the change was transient and that the future belonged to silent movies. Even the great Charlie Chaplin thought the "talkies" would soon go away. If the change points the way things are heading, you need to make a decision that will take it into account.

Step 4: Refocus all your energies on a new direction if you have concluded that the change calls for a decision. Iacocca handled this step superbly. You may remember that he promptly detected a change in his relationship with Henry Ford but delayed accepting the change. After he was fired, Iacocca was given a small office in an obscure warehouse at the Ford Motor Company until he could find a job. The humiliation he felt the morning when he entered the shabby warehouse fueled his jet-flight through steps 2, 3 and 4. In minutes, he accepted the change and realized that he didn't need to stay. By 10 a.m. he had left the place forever and in two weeks accepted the presidency of the Chrysler Corporation (1).

> ➢ Which of the four steps do you handle best?
> ➢ At which step do you delay most?

You can quicken all four steps. To quicken step 1, that is to sharpen your awareness of change, pay attention to advance signs of change and practice anticipation of change (more on that later in this chapter). If you tend to delay step 2 -- acceptance of change -- remind yourself that accepting change has nothing to do with your approval of that change at all.

Accepting change simply means not being deaf and blind to new facts that will substantially influence your life.

TO EXPEDITE STEP 3, ask yourself:

> ➢ What about this change makes me uncomfortable?
> ➢ Can I eliminate my discomfort by learning new skills?
> ➢ Can I eliminate the discomfort by changing my perspective and attitude?

Here is how it worked for my client Claire when she was desperately looking for a decision. Claire's sixteen year old daughter Carrie became pregnant and resolved to stay with her boyfriend and have the child. Claire thought Carrie was ruining her life. I introduced Claire to these lines from "The Prophet" (2):

> Your children are not your children.
> They are the sons and daughters of Life's longing for itself.
> They come through you but not from you,
> And though they are with you yet they belong not to you.
> You may give them your love but not your thoughts.
> You may house their bodies but not their souls,
> For their souls dwell in the house of tomorrow,
> which you cannot visit...
> ... seek not to make them like you.
> For life goes not backward nor tarries with yesterday.

From then on, Claire has given Carrie full emotional support. The story has a happy ending. Carrie happily married her boyfriend, and their kids delight grandparents on both sides.

If no altering of your perspective or attitude alleviates your discomfort, move to redirecting your life. To speed up step 4, unequivocally let go of the past. Like in the biblical story about leaving Sodom and Gomorra, never look back. Looking back slows down, distracts and dissipates your energies right when you need to focus on meeting new challenges. Look ahead. Ask yourself what you really want. What would bring you joy, freedom and peace. Dare to dream. Then look for ways to live your dream. More on that in chapter 10.

Signs of Upcoming Change

If you resist change, you feel discomfort. Nobody likes discomfort. Yet, it carries a precious message, "Get in tune with change."

I heard an unusual version of the Cinderella story. The stepmother was expressing love for her daughters by prompting them to get up early and work, while Cinderella was encouraged to stay in bed late and do nothing. The insidious stepmother enjoyed watching her daughters build strength by overcoming discomforts, while Cinderella grew lazy and weak. Shall we remember this story the next time a discomfort comes our way?

GRATITUDE FOR DISCOMFORT

> ➤ Recall a decision you made under the pressure of a substantial discomfort
> ➤ What did you gain from that decision?
> ➤ Were you grateful afterwards for having been "kicked" into action?

Could one be grateful for the discomfort that Conrad Hilton faced? A murderer targeted him as the next victim. Threats came from a former "angel" who had backed Hilton and his partner Powers with money for buying one of their hotels. The loan was paid back with handsome dividends. But the "angel," who had taken to heavy drinking, felt he was bilked. He shot Powers and began looking for Hilton. Not willing to live in fear, Hilton invited him for a face to face meeting. The man came and claimed that for Hilton he had no hard feelings. But when put in jail for murdering Powers, the "angel" resumed loud threats to get Hilton. Soon the Governor of Texas pardoned the murderer, and the man was about to be released. Hilton asked a priest to visit the convict in jail to reason with him. Hilton also offered an anonymous gift to help the man to a new start. What if the convict would use the gift money to buy guns? Well, Hilton did his best and now had to wait and pray. In a few days, the "angel" left Texas (3).

Each of us chooses how to respond to discomfort. Hilton chose to respond with decisions that build character and self-trust, and for that one can feel grateful. It does not take guts or intelligence to respond to discomfort with upset, anger, irritation or fear. Instead, remember that discomfort is a signal, and a valuable one. It tells you to stop resisting change. It invites you to attune to the Music of Life.

Tips on Handling Discomfort

Appreciate your discomfort and

get out of it as quickly as you can.

Avoid big discomforts by promptly handling small ones.

The Chinese say, "You can't keep birds from flying over your head, but you can keep them from making nests in your hair."

When you resist change, you feel mental, emotional and physical discomforts. The mind may reason, "However bad the familiar, at least I know what it is." The emotions -- insecurity and fear of the unknown -- join the mind in clinging to the status quo. The mind contributes such illusions as "the familiar is right" and "tradition is too strong to deviate from." They cause a feeling that the unfamiliar requires an impossible effort.

WHERE DO YOU RESIST CHANGE?

> ➤ In which area of your life do you have thoughts and feelings similar to those just described?
> ➤ Where in your life do you feel that the unfamiliar requires an impossibly big effort ?

When the emotions hate a change, the mind obligingly misinterprets even its most vociferous signs. (Remember Stalin's response to the amassing of German armies at the Soviet border.) Resistance to change creates tensions and aches in the body. Engrossed in resistance, the mind and emotions lose sight of the overall goal of health and happiness. That is what happened in 1980 when President Carter lost the election to Ronald Reagan. Rosalyn Carter could not accept their political defeat. She kept asking why people did not understand their accomplishments, how God let it happen, etc. In several months, she developed aches, pains and such stiffness that her body, as she put it, "lost all flexibility" (4).

"Flexible" means "adjustable to change, easily adaptable." Do you think it was a coincidence that Rosalyn's body grew inflexible? As she moved into a new round of decision-making -- writing a book -- she experienced healing.

When you resist change, your Body displays stagnant conditions: extra weight, constipation, loss of flexibility, swelling. In the space around you, clutter may pile up. Your Emotions display irritability and self-pity. Your Mind may indulge in finding faults in the agents of change.

SIGNS OF YOUR RESISTANCE TO CHANGE

> In which areas of your life do you have considerable discomfort – with yourself, at work, in personal relationships, finances, health, other?
> What changes have happened in that area?
> What are the signs of your resistance to change?

Before any significant change occurs,

you inner compass always notifies you.

Even in fast-paced situations one receives advance notice. A police officer, working the streets of Atlanta, wrote that when he'd answer a call, he'd know prior to arriving on the scene if he'd need a back-up unit. Before he'd turn a corner to find a man holding a revolver, this cop's body would warn him through the sensation of hair rising on the back of his neck (5).

Your Body also warns you always if you are about to create an unfavorable change. My friend Maxine had a serious car accident. Knowing how well she is aware of her body, I asked if she had had any warnings. She did. She recalled that the thought of driving to the place of her meeting made her nauseous. She thought of something else, the nausea vanished. Nevertheless she felt she could not be late for that meeting. So she started on the road, and her car was hit by a driver who crossed an intersection on the red light.

If your Emotions perceive that you are about to cause an unfavorable change, they react with negative feelings. Are those feelings always accurate? Not necessarily. Still, they are your "yellow lights," signaling that not all on your team are aligned behind your decision. Your Emotions will not help you implement it until you alter it so that your Emotions feel good about it. If you ignore the "yellow lights," the "red lights" go off – anxiety, rage, lethargy, psychosomatic illnesses.

Your Imagination offers various "yellow light" warnings. While you are previewing an option, unpleasant images might pop up. Pay attention, as my client Brandon did. He received a flattering offer to enter into a business partnership with Arnold. Brandon got excited. Yet, he noticed that thoughts about partnership with Arnold triggered in him images of disasters and failures. Heeding those warnings, Brandon investigated the matter further. New facts confirmed that Brandon would be better off to stay clear of Arnold.

Here is another area of preliminary warnings issued by your Imagination. If someone's image – your subordinate's, child's, spouse's – upsets you (for instance, triggers judgments or anger), when you meet them, a conflict may arise. To avoid conflict, bring yourself into balance before meeting them.

Your Unconscious and Coach bring you precognitive dreams. People who keep dream journals over extended periods of time attest that all major changes in one's life are previewed and "rehearsed" in dreams. That help us handle change (6). For instance, as a boy, Neil Armstrong, the first man to walk on the moon, had a recurrent dream where he'd hover over the ground. There was no end to that dream (7).

Sometimes during the day, when you are preoccupied with what seems urgent, you may suddenly feel very drowsy. If you take a nap, a dream may show you a shortcut to your goal or call your attention to something you have overlooked that must be handled. Such a nap requires only minutes. Unfortunately, we usually grab a cup of coffee instead.

What do you do when you have warned your loved one many times of upcoming trouble, and s/he does not respond? You'd probably want to grab his or her attention somehow. That is what your Unconscious does. If you keep missing or ignoring warnings, your Unconscious may bring you nightmares. Some people ignore them too, and then run into accidents, disease, financial trouble. All in all, you are given plenty of advance notice of upcoming changes.

> *If a change startles you, either you did not pay attention or you chose to ignore all the warnings.*

Five Secrets of Right Timing

When you are in tune with change, your timing is right and you find yourself in the right place at the right time. You keep in tune with change by following your inner compass. It means you respond to signals of change your team broadcasts. The secret of right timing is your prompt response to change. To fine-tune your timing we add one more step that precedes the other steps of the beginning phase -- anticipation of change.

> *It is too late to recognize change when it has already occurred. Anticipate change by "tuning into the future."*

You can do that by letting your Imagination lead the team, as did Bill Walton, a player of a championship basketball team. On the night before a game he'd analyze carefully the team and the player against whom he was to play. On the day of the game he'd refresh himself with a nap and then take two and a half hours exclusively to tune into the upcoming game. Sitting in his hotel room, he'd feel the rhythm of the game, its tempo and its movement. He'd anticipate possible maneuvers of the players in such detail that in his imagination he saw even the spin of the ball. Later on the court he moved with utmost precision and confidence because he had already seen it all, had made that move, or blocked that shot (8).

Situations on the basketball court change in a fraction of a second. If one can anticipate such rapid change, you can anticipate upcoming changes in your life. The imagination is not the exclusive property of a few, but your window into the future -- a personal "crystal ball" each of us has. You are welcome to thrive on its magic powers. To become adept in anticipating change, give yourself regularly, as did Bill Walton, a gift of time when you anticipate probable changes and play out scenarios of your successful responses.

Anticipation of change is not a mental calculation. All mental analysis of the situation is done beforehand. Bill Walton's anticipation was done out of his love and feel for basketball. Anticipation of change works best when you do it out of

love for yourself, others and the flow of life. Of course, anticipating change has as much to do with provoking anxiety about
your future as a raincoat hanging in your closet with provoking
rain.

To sum up, these are the five steps of the beginning phase:
anticipate change, become aware of it, accept it, sense its trend
and if needed, refocus on a new direction.

PREPARE TO HANDLE AN UPCOMING CHANGE

> ➤ In your journal, list noteworthy changes in yourself, in
>   significant people in your life, in your circumstances
> ➤ Which change concerns you most?
> ➤ What about this change concerns you most?
> ➤ What is the trend of this change?
> ➤ If you don't sense the trend, think of probable scenarios
> ➤ What is your favorite scenario?
> ➤ What can you do to bring it about?
> ➤ What is the worst scenario?
> ➤ What would be your ideal response to it?
> ➤ Imagine scenes where you respond to the worst sce-
>   nario to your full satisfaction. To gain cooperation of
>   your Emotions *make sure to imagine the feeling you
>   want to have while handling this scenario.*

As was mentioned in chapter 4, what you keep in your
Imagination, your Unconscious takes as a blueprint to implement. As you keep imagining yourself aptly adapting to
change, the Unconscious feeds energy into that.

Each time you imagine yourself well adapting to change,
healthy neurological and other adjustments take place, preparing your inner compass team to handle change well. The fun
and joy of these imaginings indicate that your Coach contributes energy to keeping you in-tune with change.

Signs of Upcoming Change That Are Unique to You.

Have you ever been taken aback by change? The following exercise lets you extract great value from those experiences. Since your Imagination is not time-bound, by playing back a past situation, you can detect *now* the warnings you missed before. You may feel resistant to doing this exercise. It's natural. None of us is anxious to review what we didn't do well. Bypass resistance and have fun.

MAKE A "FILE" OF PAST WARNINGS

> ➤ Recall a specific situation where a change shocked you
> ➤ Which signals that the change was coming did you ignore?
> ➤ What caused you to ignore them?
> ➤ To discover warnings you had missed, let your Imagination play back that period of your life. Relax, sit back and watch it as you do in a movie theater. No popcorn though, since you want all your attention focused on the feedback you will be receiving from your Body, Emotions, and Mind while you watch the movie. Watch the movie a few times if necessary. At a certain point, you will start picking up your players' responses. It might be a strange feeling, vague discomfort, tension, pain, concern, an image, whatever.
> ➤ List in your journal the warnings you noticed
> ➤ Had you acknowledged those signals as warnings, what and how could you have done better?
> ➤ How will you use the insights you've just gained?

The aim of this exercise is to make you aware of the warning signals available to you and to sensitize you to more subtle clues that quicken decisions. What if you are not aware of any clues? You can solicit them from your Coach right now.

How? Simply relax, then say, "I ask for the awareness of the clues in such and such area of my concern!" Then observe changes in your Body sensations, Imagination and Emotions.

> *Change, even when it appears disastrous, gives us an opportunity to let go of whatever clutters the body and mind, house and relationships, files and unconscious. When we truly accept change, we discover that its meaning is.*
> *Cleansing Healing Announcing New Glorious Ecstasy.*

Summary

No substantial change is ever sudden. Your entire inner compass team notifies you of upcoming change in numerous ways. Respond to your team's signals immediately. Then your timing will be right and you can enjoy new opportunities.

Now you are ready for the central phase of decision-making which is the topic of the next chapter.

10

How to Recognize
People and Goals
Worth Your Commitment

This chapter is about the central phase of multiphase decisions. Here you will discover a tool for making instant decisions, that is unique to you, and apply this tool to recognize people and goals worth your commitment.

Are You on the Right Track?

When you start the central phase, the rhythm of decision-making changes from "the faster-the-better" to that of quiet soul-searching. First, ask yourself, What do I long for in the depth of my being? Jot down your answer. The first answer rarely reveals one's bottom-line truth. For instance, many say, "I want a million dollars." But in itself a million dollars is a pile of paper. What people really want is what they hope this money will bring. That differs for different people. What is it for you? Security? Recognition? Independence? Whatever it is, the money symbolizes the experience that makes people feel full and complete, that is the experience of fulfillment. We humans want fulfillment. That is why,

> *a goal is right for you if its achieving brings you fulfillment*

Unlike gratification, fulfillment upgrades your self-image.

Fulfillment versus gratification.

While gratification entices you, it steals your freedom and peace. For instance, a spicy meal may be gratifying but after it, your Body craves drinks and sweets and that craving pulls on you. Another example would be possessive emotional love. It vacillates between the pleasures of possession and sharp stings of jealousy and fear. Similarly, compulsive attention-getting produces "highs" and then inevitable "lows." All in all, gratification does not reduce cravings and desires that pull on you incessantly as though you were shackled to an invisible pendulum that forever oscillates, depriving you of your freedom of choice, rushing you away from the equilibrium of inner peace.

Can it be otherwise? Certainly. A balanced peaceful meal supplies you with energy without causing cravings. Unconditional loving -- loving out of the sheer joy of loving, without expecting anything in return – gives your and your loved ones the freedom of choice. It deepens your peace. A fulfilling experience, even as simple as skipping an ice cream, imparts a good "clean" feeling. When you manage to quit drinking or overeating, when you drop the habit of reacting with irritation or anger or when you otherwise take charge of your life, you experience fulfillment. It builds self-trust.

Betty Ford, the former first lady, offers as good an example as any. Two days after her return from a drug and alcohol rehabilitation program in California, she had to fly to New York to host a dinner for dignitaries. Alone in a New York hotel room, she felt nervous and insecure. She knew that a bit of martini would quickly restore her badly needed confidence. And here it was -- right in front of her -- a big pitcher of martinis obligingly brought to her hotel room. Nobody would have guessed had she taken a bit from that big pitcher. Except, she would know. She chose to pass up the drink. Her reward was new confidence and self-trust (1).

Any fulfilling experience strengthens, stabilizes, and lifts you without binding you to the "high-low" vacillation of the pendulum. A fulfilling experience is graced with such perfection that you would not want to change anything in it. So let's discover what fulfills you.

Your Personal Tool
for Making Instant Decisions

What fulfills you? The real answer to this question is usually buried under layers of conditioning. The following exercise was designed to unearth your answer. Do this pleasant exercise now. Or, read the entire chapter, then come back and do the exercise. But by all means do it, for it reveals a unique-to-you tool for making decisions with ease and speed. This tool will help you set goals, recognize right-for-you people and make other important decisions. So find a quiet place and make sure you will not be disturbed. In your journal write your answer to each question in the exercise. This writing is for you; nobody else needs to see it. Create a space within yourself where you feel safe to communicate with yourself. Suspend judgments and any attempts to censor. Write honestly what is true for you. If you answered any of the following questions before, do it anew, from the space you are in now.

1. Start daydreaming. Or, begin imagining a pleasant scene. For instance: You are lying on lush summer grass. Nothing

and nobody can disturb you. (An angel took all the bugs for a vacation.) Luxuriate in the fragrance of flowers, feel the caressing touch of a slight breeze, enjoy the serenity of the white clouds in the sky. Or, you are being cradled by warm ocean waves. (Do you hear the surf and the seagulls?) Or, you are enthralled by the fire in a fireplace, listening to the crackling, feeling the warmth, smelling the burning wood. Or, through the window of a warm cabin you are marveling at snowflakes gently descending to the ground, covering trees and bushes. (Do you hear the silence?) Enjoy the scene you have chosen until a pleasant reverie starts. Let the reverie take you wherever it will.

    a. While you were daydreaming, what was your most beautiful experience?

    b. What quality of it made it fulfilling for you?
Underline your answer to the last question.

2. Assume that by the time of your death, you will have accomplished everything you wanted. With this in mind:

    a. List two things you'd like to accomplish before you die. Choose any one of them.

    b. What about it makes you feel full and complete? Keep asking this question.
Underline your last answer.

For instance, one of the things Roger, an engineer and inventor, wants to accomplish is to leave his son Eric a substantial inheritance. Question: What is fulfilling about leaving Eric this inheritance? Roger's answer: It should ease Eric's life. Question: What about making Eric's life easier is fulfilling for you? Roger's answer: I'd feel that as a father I've met my obligations. Question: What about meeting those obligations makes you feel full and complete? Roger: I feel freer. My inner freedom expands, and that makes me feel full and complete. Roger underlines the last answer.

    c Again, assuming that you have accomplished what you wanted before you died, write a brief obituary for yourself. How would you want to be remembered? What is fulfilling about that? <u>Underline.</u>

    d. What was the most fulfilling experience of your life? (if no real experience comes to Mind, imagine one). What made it fulfilling? <u>Underline.</u>

3. If you had all the time and money you wanted, what would you be doing? What is fulfilling in doing that? <u>Underline this answer.</u>

4. Explore your image of success:

    a. Who is your ideal of success? It can be a person, a combination of several people, a historical figure, a fantasy. What about him/her makes him/her your ideal successful person? What in his/her experiences do you find fulfilling? <u>Underline.</u>

    b. List what every successful person would do, be, have. What do you find fulfilling about doing, being, having that? <u>Underline this answer</u>.

    c. What would <u>you</u> need to accomplish in order to accept -- beyond the shadow of a doubt -- that <u>you</u> are a success. What do you find fulfilling in accomplishing that? <u>Underline this answer</u>.

    d. What must be present in you and/or in your life in order for you to acknowledge yourself as a success? What about it is fulfilling? <u>Underline this answer.</u>

5. Explore these aspects of relating to yourself:

    a. What would make you love yourself most?

    b. What about it makes you feel full and complete?

    c. What would make you appreciate yourself most?

d. What would it be like to love and appreciate yourself fully?

e. What is fulfilling in that? <u>Underline your answer</u>.

6. Review your underlined answers. Which qualities of experience recur most often? Of these, which ones brings you
most fulfillment ?

Sometimes, a single unifying thread runs through the entire exercise, and the quality that makes your experience fulfilling clearly stands out. We will use the abbreviation FQ for
fulfilling quality. More often, several qualities come up. If this
is your case, do the exercise again. Why? Because past conditionings bury your innermost yearnings like petrified soil. Each
time you do the exercise, it loosens and mellows the soil, letting your deeper truth surface.

You may have noticed that when you do this exercise,
your energy increases as if you are tapping a source of energy.
Indeed, you are. And when you hit your bottom-line answer,
that is, when you find your current FQ, your energy shoots up
as if you have accessed an ocean of energy, whereas before you
were accessing only rivers.

FQ varies from person to person. Here are examples of
FQs: *Peace, Self-Trust, Clarity, Gratitude, Full Presence*, (full
attention on the present with the attitude of "I'd rather be here
than anywhere else"), Joy, *Freedom, Fun, Aliveness, Self-
Loving* (loving yourself no matter how you perform, no matter
what others think, feel, or say about you), *Taking Charge of
Your Life, Being True To Yourself.*

Make sure you verbalize your FQ carefully so that it accu-
rately expresses your inner experience of fulfillment. You may
capture that experience in one word ("peace"), a phrase (
"dancing with Spirit," "trail-blazing,") or an affirmation (e.g., "

I am moving through life with the laugh in my belly.") Some connect with their FQ through a command, like "Be still and know that I am God." The qualities which make experiences fulfilling are the qualities of your Coach. Discovering your FQ lets you know through which quality of experience you best resonate with your Coach and open yourself to intuition.

> *Often, it is not the quality of experience but attaining more of this quality that makes the experience fulfilling, for instance, it is expanding of freedom rather than freedom itself.*

Check whether you linked your fulfillment to someone else's approval or happiness. If you did:

> ➤ Recall a situation where you linked your fulfillment to someone's approval or happiness. Let your Imagination play back the situation.
> ➤ What did you feel when you got their approval?
> ➤ What about it made you feel full and complete?
> ➤ What does his/her approval or happiness give you (security, loving, sense of being worthy, etc.)?
> ➤ How can you provide for yourself what they give you?

This example of Ray, a school principal, illustrates that what you want for others usually mirrors what you want for yourself. If Ray had all the time and money he wanted, he'd open a school where each student would be taught to value himself and his uniqueness. Ray's ideal of success is a teacher who makes his students aware that each of them really counts. For Ray, success is lifting people in their own eyes. He felt fulfilled when he felt worthy of love and respect. Ray gathered that his fulfilling quality was self-worth/self-appreciation. Ray's wish for others to feel worthy characteristically reflects what he yearns for himself – a knowing that he is a worthwhile person. Another example. Desperately wanting someone else's love mirrors how desperately one needs the comfort of his/her own love.

Make sure that you end up with one FQ. If, after doing the exercise several times, you ended with two qualities, do this:
> Identify with, i.e., become, one of the qualities you are choosing from. Then identify with the other one
> Which one would you rather be?
> Which of the two qualities relaxes you more, energizes you more, makes you breathe easier? That one is a better candidate for your FQ

Your FQ reflects your powerful innermost drive. If, during the exercise, you become impatient, you are likely to mistake a creek, a smaller current for the inner stream of success.

> *Impatience is a form of resistance by which the inertia of this planet holds us captive.*

Keep doing the exercise over and over until you feel you have discovered your bottom-line FQ. Your stream of success is there, waiting to be discovered.

<u>ANCHORING YOUR FQ.</u>

1. Identify with PEACE this way:
    a. Exhale tensions, worries, concerns -- inhale PEACE. Do that a few times
    b. Take time to imbue each part, system, organ, and cell of your Body from nose to toes with PEACE
    c. Now imagine PEACE filling up other players, first, your Imagination, then your Emotions, then your Mind and, finally, your Unconscious

       d. Get used to being PEACE. Remember to sit, stand, eat, listen and move as PEACE

2. PEACE helps achieve your goal

       a. What is the main obstacle to achieving your current goal? What worries you about it?

       b. Become PEACE. How does PEACE view the obstacle and your worries about it?

       c. How has PEACE helped you use your obstacle to propel yourself to your goal?

3. Replace PEACE with your FQ and repeat the exercise

How to Use Your Tool to Recognize the Right People

To check whether a particular person is right for you, do this:

1 Get in touch with your FQ by recalling an instance when you have experienced it. Relive the experience of fulfillment. It will be a reference point for the next step

2. Imagine situations where you will interact with this person and pay attention to what's happening with your FQ. Is it expanding and deepening? Or, has it vanished? If your fulfillment increases, you have got a "yes' vote for that person. If it decreases, it is a "no" vote.

Here is an example. Martha and her partner Bob, a biochemist, struggled for 16 years to develop and market their environmentally safe cleaning products, At first, the demand was rising slowly. Then it skyrocketed, and Martha found herself pressured from many directions. Should she build a new plant, modernize the old one or transfer the production overseas? Bob left to do research in another field, and Martha found herself dealing with hundreds of new people. She urgently needed a capable administrative assistant. Her newspaper ad pulled 23 applicants. She selected the three most qualified – Ben, a college graduate, keenly interested in business, Norma, the former secretary of Martha's retired friend, and Irene, a former high school teacher. To choose among them, Martha used her FQ which was deepening her inner peace. It took her less than a minute to decide to hire Irene. Quiet, unassuming and intelligent Irene proved to be an excellent choice. How did Martha know to choose Irene? Martha imagined first, Norma, then Irene, and then Ben at her side, in her hectic and demanding life. Irene's presence deepened Martha's inner peace most.

To Commit or not to commit.

As was mentioned, a goal is right for you if it brings you fulfillment. But that criterion alone is not enough. A goal may be great, but do you desire it so strongly that you will stretch beyond your present comfort zones? Will you sacrifice your inadequacies that get in the way of achieving this goal? In other words, are you willing to commit to this goal 100%? This criterion is vital: *a right goal warrants your full commitment.*

Those who have reached the "unreachable stars" have chosen a goal which brings them fulfillment *and* have kept full commitment until the goal is won. Nancy Foreman is one of those people. She grew up in a small Nebraska town that lacked even indoor plumbing. But she longed for what she called "life unlimited" -- a fulfilling experience of personal growth amid a stream of top achievers. What outer goal would enhance her fulfillment? She could become a psychologist specializing in peak performers, an author writing about top achievers, an entrepreneur, etc. Nancy singled out a career in TV. When she set that goal, few saw it as realistic: at the time she was a 36-year-old mother of two, on the brink of divorce, with no money or connections. But she dared to commit to her fulfillment and, despite many obstacles, did become a life-style correspondent for the NBC "Today Show" in New York (2).

> *Only the goal to which you commit 100% is worth going for.*

What if you are partially committed? Then your players are unsure whether they are in or out of the Game. As they loiter, frittering away time and energy, inertia takes over. Your Body grows sluggish, Emotions turn irritable and unstable, Imagination dwells on distractions and worries, and your Mind meanders. Incompletions pile up, causing your Unconscious to reject new ideas, approaches and people who are different. All in all, partial commitment debases your inner compass team.

> *Partial commitment detracts from your health, wealth, and happiness much more than you realize.*

Conversely, full commitment erases all excuses for not doing your best. 100% commitment puts all your players on the line, along with your self-respect and self-trust. You clear up incompletions. Your Mind organizes resources to support your goal; your Emotions light up with enthusiasm; your Imagination feasts on your inner and outer goals; your Body shapes up. You learn new skills, become ingenious, persuasive, indefatigable. Rain or shine, you are quick to get up in the morning. You use each obstacle as a springboard to better solutions. As your actions demonstrate full commitment consistently, a new, special relationship with your goal develops -- your goal starts pulling you toward itself. That is what happened with Jackie Robinson. Back in 1943, when Branch Rickey, then President of the Dodgers, set out to bring African-Americans into the then all-white major league baseball, he searched for a man who, amid infuriating unwarranted hostility, would not only excel in sports but also maintain the image of a fine gentleman. The choice fell on Jackie Robinson. Many times during incidents of abuse, humiliation, threats to his family, and physical assaults, he was ready to explode with rage. He believed in swift retaliation, and in the past had been known to fight for his dignity over and over. But had he exploded now, the headlines would surely have publicized it as an "ugly racial incident." Once he fully committed himself to breaking the color barrier in major league baseball, his goal -- not his past -- molded his decisions. At decision points, his goal inspired him not to strike back but demonstrate day in and day out, year after year supreme human and athletic qualities (3).

Full commitment is the zestful way of your Coach. "The moment one definitely commits oneself, Providence moves too ... raising in one's favor... material assistance, which no man could have dreamed would have come his way."(4) "Whatever you can do, or dream you can, begin it. Boldness has genius, power and magic in it. Begin it now." (5)

How to sustain your full commitment.

Have you ever committed to a goal but later lost your enthusiasm and never reached the goal? It is not easy to remain committed when other obligations pull on you and distractions and obstacles pop up. But if you could re-fuel your commitment, what exciting goals you could reach!

Now you can re-fuel. How? Whenever you feel dejected or need a boost, evoke an experience of fulfillment. Fulfillment recharges you with enthusiasm and energy. Fulfillment makes you -- once again -- ready to play the Game of Life.

> *By identifying with your FQ you evoke a fulfilling experience and access your Coach's energy and enthusiasm.*

The above paragraph offers you a powerful way to sustain full commitment. However, just reading about it is not enough. To actually sustain full commitment, engage your entire team in the identification process as often as you can through your favorites among the following exercises.

TO IDENTIFY WITH YOUR FQ:

Replace PEACE, used here as an example, with your FQ.

1. Recall an occasion when you experienced PEACE. Relive it. At the peak of your experience of PEACE, note which parts of your Body have received PEACE

2. Let your Imagination empty you, washing away worries and concerns, then let it fill you up with PEACE. Drink PEACE as nectar.

3. Hear PEACE as a rich and sublime sound filling you up and resonating with your entire being.

4. Smell PEACE as a fragrance emanating from your heart.

5. During the day ask yourself, "Do I sit as PEACE? Do I walk as PEACE? Do I listen to people as PEACE?"

6. Which symbols evoke in you the experience of PEACE? Surround yourself with those symbols.

7. For 33 days, before going to sleep, experience this: "What was before was before. From now on, I am PEACE. Inside of me is a world of PEACE, and I am its center. As I become still, the Universe of PEACE opens to me its countless faces and facets. As I become still, I know how to live this moment as one of PEACE. When still, I discover how to resolve conflicts in ways that deepen my peace. What was before was before. From now on, I am PEACE." Note: Rather than "I am peaceful," affirm, "I am PEACE."

8. For 33 days, every evening, ask yourself, "What have I learned about PEACE today? In your journal write a one sentence answer.

By regularly identifying with your FQ you align with your Coach, breakthrough to freedom and initiate yourself into decision-making mastery.

How to select the right strategy

The major criterion for selecting goals applies to selecting strategies. Right-for-you strategy brings you fulfillment.

> *When you select goals and strategies by the same criteria,*
> *you integrate your inner compass team.*

If you select a strategy which by its nature contradicts your goal, your players get confused and cannot perform well. For example, the goal of peace requires that all your players align with peace. What about fighting for peace? Can we achieve peace through violence? Violence requires that all your players align with violence. Since we humans have a long history of wars, we tend to think that we have no other options and must resort to violence. Apparently, our ancestors thought the same way about cannibalism and slavery. We abolished both, and now, even when very hungry, we don't eat each other's bodies for dinner. And we also manage without slaves. If we entirely abolish violence, we may be able -- through our ingenuity and creativity -- to find peaceful ways out of any conflict -- personal, group, or international. Harbingers of the new, nonviolent era have set inspiring precedents: Gandhi peacefully led India to freedom from foreign rule; Kenyatta did the same for Kenya, and Martin Luther King, even in acute racial conflicts, used only peaceful means.

> *If you resort to a strategy that by its nature contradicts*
> *your goal, you are not fully committed to your goal.*

Full commitment, however, is not an optional but an absolute criterion for a right-for-you goal.

In the central phase, we follow two great ancient commandments: "Man, know thyself" and "To thine own self be true." In regard to the latter, people frequently say: "If I act on my truth, if I do what is right for me, others will feel hurt, and I do not want to hurt." If this issue comes up for you, ask yourself, "Has my concern about not hurting others turned into an excuse for not living a life of integrity?" If so, your strategy was self-defeating. When you fail to act on your truth, a feeling of self-betrayal settles in. You have betrayed your inner knowing; you have betrayed what you knew as truth. Conversely, when you follow your truth, you set yourself free, and for others you blaze a trail to freedom.

Summary

A goal is right for you if you commit to it 100% and if it brings you fulfillment. Once you discover specifically what fulfills you, you gain a personal tool for making instant decisions and choosing people and goals worth your commitment.

Epilogue:

How to Stop Worrying *about* Making a Wrong Decision

In decision-making you move from the familiar to the unknown via an unfamiliar route -- without a map. It means that you will inevitably make wrong turns.

> *If you think you can go through life without making wrong decisions, you are on the wrong planet. Here, people learn from mistakes. When you have made enough wrong decisions to grow – not cringe – from them, you become a respected and sought after person of experience.*

For the sake of brevity, let us lump what you would call a "mistake," "failure," or a "wrong decision" into one term "mistake." Now remember: decision-making is your Game of Life. Can a game remain a game without mistakes? Imagine how much fun and suspense would be lost! So mistakes are an integral and valuable part of decision-making. They serve the overall purpose of the Game – the purpose of anchoring your inner peace, freedom and joy so well that they become your normal state. Facing your terrible mistake affords you a training ground to practice and deepen your joy, freedom and peace. Facing your mistake also gives you a golden opportunity to look at yourself and the world with new eyes. Columbus discovered America by mistake. How can your mistake lead you to your America?

How to Benefit Immediately from Your Mistake

If you are so upset with your mistake that you cannot stand it another minute, take a nice deep breath. For ten breaths -- ten inhales and ten exhales -- focus on your breathing. Starting with the fourth breath, on each inhale and each exhale, say inwardly. "Yes!" "Yes" to the new and valuable aspect of yourself you will discover through this mistake. "Yes" to a deeper joy, peace and freedom waiting for you.

Now you may want to use the following exercise to benefit from your "awful" mistake.

BENEFIT FROM YOUR RECENT MISTAKE/ WRONG DECISION

1. What would you view as a right behavior in the situation where , in your opinion, you made a mistake?
2. Put the essence of the right behavior in no more than 12 words, starting with "I am..." The shorter the affirmation, the clearer the essence of your right behavior stands out.
3. Let your Imagination play out your right behavior. See it, hear it, feel it, taste it, smell it.
4. Forgive yourself for all the judgments you have made about yourself and others related to this mistake.

A mistake may pave the way to greater opportunities, even save your life. A story is told about a man who missed his flight and with it his best deal. He was ready to kill himself. Then he learned that the plane he missed exploded in the air leaving no survivors.

5. List three opportunities this mistake has opened up for you. What have you learned from this mistake that can bless your life and the lives of others?

6. Act on at least one new opportunity immediately.

"Immediately" is the key word here, because when your Mind judges that you made a mistake, that upsets your Emotions, which in turn upset your Body. That keeps three of your players stuck in the past and not available for your present game.

7. Be grateful for what you've learned and for what you're about to receive.

If there is no time for all seven steps, simply affirm to yourself, "Next time I'll do better," and play out in your Imagination what that "better" is like.

There is a value in each experience. If you have received the value, it means you have turned your mistake into your treasure. So, do not block yourself with labels like "mistake." Remind yourself that even the most disastrous decisions yield value and learning. Make sure to turn your mistakes into your treasures quickly. "Suffering takes time" (John-Roger). If you have time to suffer over a mistake, you are not moving fast enough. When you do, no picture behind the window – ugly or beautiful -- can occupy your attention for too long.

> *If you are not making mistakes, it is a warning sign of not venturing outside your comfort zone, of not making enough decisions and not allowing enough newness into your life.*

Support yourself well when facing your mistake.

We make mistakes in the areas where, metaphorically speaking, we are learning to walk. What do you do when a

211

baby falls and hurts himself? You pick him up, love and encourage. When you discover that you've made a mistake, you also need love and encouragement *from yourself.*

If -- at the critical moment of facing up to your awful mistake -- you have managed to love yourself more than ever, you have truly benefited from your mistake.

How to use this book to find your next step.

After you have read this book and used the inner compass techniques in your daily life, test out the following. Whenever you need help with a decision, simply open this book at random, read and do whatever is suggested until you know your next step. It will not take you long to get your answers.

You have come to the end of this book. If you practiced its techniques, you have magnified your power of making quick decisions. Immeasurably more of your power is still dormant, waiting to be activated. To bring it into play, take every opportunity to make decisions through your inner compass. Each time you do, you gain more skills and power to triumph over obstacles and deepen your joy, freedom, and peace.

Welcome to the Game!

ENDNOTES

Chapter One
1. Jonathan Roberts, *Decision-Making During International Crises*, St. Martin,1988
2. John Arnold, *Make Up Your Mind*, AMACON, 1979

Chapter Two
1. Piero Ferrucci, *What We May Be,* J.P. Tarcher, 1982
2. Beryl Markham, *West with the Night*, North Point Press, 1983

Chapter Three
1. Beryl Markham, *West with the Night*, North Point Press, 1983
2. Michio Kushi, *Natural Healing through Macrobiotics*, Japan Publications, 1978
3. Jeanne Achterberg, *Imagery In Healing,* New Science Library, 1985
4. Yogi Ramacharaka, *The Hindu-Yogi Breathing Exercises*, Yoga Publications, 1976
5. Reshad Field, *The Last Barrier*, Harper & Row, 1977
6. Moshe Feldenkreis, *Awareness Through Movement,* Harper & Row, 1977
7. Louise Hay, *You Can Heal Your Life,* Hay House, CA,1996
8. as quoted in: Kathleen Krull, *12 Keys to Writing Books that Sell,* Writer's Digest, 1989

Chapter Four
1. Horace Judson, *In Search for Solutions*, Holt, Rinehart & Winston, 1980
2. Nicola Tesla, *My Inventions*, Hart Brothers, Williston, Vermont, 1982 (originally published in *Electrical Experimenter,* 1919)

Endnotes

3. O.C. Simonton, S. Matthews-Simonton, J. Creighton, *Getting Well Again*, Bantam, 1980
4. Jeanne Achterberg, *Imagery in Healing*, New Science Library, 1985
5. Maxwell Maltz, *Psycho-cybernetics*, A Fireside Book, Simon and Schuster,1960
6. Brigid Keenan, *Dior in Vogue,* Harmony Books, 1981
7. A. Schwarzenegger, D. Hall, *ARNOLD: The Education of a Bodybuilder,* Pocket Books, 1985
8. Mary Lou Retton and Bela Karolyi, Mary Lou, *Creating an Olympic Champion*, McGraw, 1985
9. Shakti Gawain, *Creative Visualization*, Bantam, 1985

Chapter Five
1. Jimmy Carter, *Keeping Faith, Memoirs of a President,* Bantam Books, 1982
2. S. Mathews-Simonton, O.C. Simonton, J.Creighton, *Getting Well Again,* Bantam, 1984
3. Melvin Helitzer, *Comedy Writing Secrets, How to Think Funny,* Writer's Digest, 1987
4. John-Roger, *Are You Doing Negative Meditation?* audiotape, MSIA, P.O.B 513935, Los Angeles, CA 90051-1935
5. David Burns, *Feeling Good*, William Morrow, 1980
6. Ken Keyes, Jr. with Penny Keyes, *A Conscious Person's Guide to Relationships*, Living Love Publications, 1979
7. John-Roger , Peter McWilliams, *You Can't Afford the Luxury of a Negative Thought*, Prelude Press, 1988
8. D. Greenburg, M. Jacobs, *How to Make Yourself Miserable,* Random House, 1966

Chapter Six
1. Betty Edwards, *Drawing on the Right Side of the Brain,* Jeremy Tarcher, 1979
2. Betty Ford, *A Glad Awakening*, Doubleday, 1987

3. Harold Greenwald with Elizabeth Rich, *The Happy Person*, Avon Books, 1984
4. Martin Seligman, *Learned Optimism*, A. Knopf, 1990
5. David Burns, *Feeling Good*, Signet Book, 1980
6. John-Roger and Peter McWilliams, *You Cannot Afford the Luxury of a Negative Thought*, Prelude Press, 1988
7. George Soros, *Soros on Soros*, John Wiley & Sons, 1995
8. John-Roger, *Precipitation: Manifesting Abundance*, audio tape, MSIA, P.O.B 513935, Los Angeles, CA 90051-1935
9. Paul Getty, *How to Be Rich*, Jove Books, New York, 1983

Chapter Seven
1. John-Roger, *The Way Out,* audiotape, 1982, distributed by Carmel Sounds, 620 14th St., Virginia Beach, VA 23451
2. Elsie Sechrist, Dreams, *Your Magic Mirror*, Warner Books, 1974

Chapter Eight
1. Nicholas von Hoffman, *The Washington Post*, 7/21/ 1971
2. E. Poesnecker, *It's Only Natural*, Adventures Publ., 1975
3. *Philadelphia Inquirer* of June 3d & June 11th, 1989
4. The New Encyclopedia *Britannica*, v.9, 1985
5. Alec Guinness, *Blessings in Disguise*, A. Knopf, 1986
6. "Sir Alec Guinness" in *Current Biographies*, 1981.
7. Horace Judson, *The Search for Solutions*, Holt, Reinhart & Winston, 1980
8. John-Roger, *Inner Worlds of Meditation,* Mandeville Press, CA, 1997
9. Isaac Asimov, *"The Eureka Phenomenon,"* in *The Norton Reader*, W.W. Norton & Company, 1977
10. C.P. Snow, *The Search*, Scribner, 1959
11. Ray Rowan, *The Intuitive Manager*, Berkley Books, 1987
12. Mary Kay Ash, *Mary Kay*, Barnes and Noble Books, 1981
13. Nathan Sharansky, *Fear Not Evil*, Random House, 1988
14. Linda Lee, *The Man Only I Knew*, Warner Paperback, 1975

Endnotes

15. W. Harman and H. Rheingold, *Higher Creativity*, Jeremy Tarcher, 1984
16. Edgar Mitchell, Ph.D., *New Frontier*, Jan/Feb. 1991
17. John-Roger, *Finding and Directing Creativity*, audiotape, MSIA, P.O. Box 513950, Los Angeles, CA 90051-1935

Chapter Nine
1. Lee Iacocca with William Novak, *IACOCCA,* An autobiography, Bantam Books, 1986
2. Kahlil Gibran, *The Prophet*, A. Knopf, 1976
3. Conrad Hilton, *Be My Guest*, Prentice-Hall, 1957
4. Jimmy and Rosalyn Carter, *Everything to Gain*, Random House, 1981
5. W. Allen Anderson, *"The Spiritual Side of Police Work,"* New Frontier, Jan. 1987
6. Elsie Sechrist, *Dreams, Your Magic Mirror*, Warner Books, 1974
7. Neil Armstrong, M.Collins, E.Aldrin, *First on the Moon*, Little, Brown & Co, Boston, 1970
8. David Halberstam, *The Breaks In the Game*, A. Knopf, 1981

Chapter Ten
1. Betty Ford, Betty: *A Glad Awakening*, Doubleday, 1987
2. Nancy Foreman, *Bound For Success*, Simon and Schuster, 1985
3. Jackie Robinson with A. Duckett, *I Never Had It Made*, Putnam, 1972
4. W.H. Murray, as quoted in John-Roger and Peter McWilliams, *Life 101*, Prelude Press, 1990
5. Goethe, as quoted in John-Roger and Peter McWilliams, *Life 101*, Prelude Press, 1990

INDEX

Index

Acknowledgments

It is my great pleasure to thank all the people who contributed to making this book possible. John-Roger has inspired and encouraged me from the start of this project. John Soellner introduced me to the classics and rare gems of marketing. Judy Appelbaum and Florence Janovic helped me gain insights into publishing. Stede Barber demystified the design and production phases for me. Kathy Dolan has always found the time to listen to different versions of the text, to give me her intelligent remarks and proofread several incarnations of the manuscript. Charles Lerman, Ph.D., Betsy Washburne, and Jackie Goodman also generously gave their time to proofread the manuscript. Jane Packman patiently answered my questions about the peculiarities of the English language. Rosalind Leighton contributed her expertise as a superb reference librarian. Brittany Walls added her graceful artistic touch to chart 1.1. My warm thanks go also to Mark Rohland, Ph.D. of Bryn Mawr College and Andree Leighton of Temple University for their keen comments and encouragement, as well as to Miriam Seidel for her suggestions and connections. My gratitude goes to Nelly Tsivina, Ph.D. for her much appreciated practical help, as well as to Amiran Elwork, Ph.D. and Polly Memhard who shared with me keys to their publishing successes. To all my clients and other fine people who helped me along the way I extend my heartfelt thanks .

A very special gratitude and appreciation goes to my husband Lev for his love and support and to my daughter Irina whose loving strength and independence helped me complete the book.

About the Author

International educator, Zelma Barinov, Ph.D., has been exploring decision-making for over 25 years. She received her doctorate in Information Science and Cybernetics in Moscow (Russia). She then headed a department at a research center, taught postgraduate students, published 25 scientific monographs and developed a new approach to making decisions in times of fast, unpredictable change. In 1975 she emigrated to the United States. Now a successful consultant in the US and Europe, she coaches entrepreneurs, leading decision-makers from Fortune 500 corporations, government facilities, academia, as well as individuals in all walks of life.